Dictionary of International Business Law

DICTIONARY OF INTERNATIONAL Business Law

LUCAS OTTO

GLOBAL
professional
publishing

Global Professional Publishing Limited
The European Innovation Centre
Fitzroy House
11 Chenies Street
London WC1E 7EY

ISBN: 978-0-85297-658-6

Typeset by Kevin O'Connor

Printed in the United States of America
by Integrated Book Technology

Preface

Our business world is so open and so transparent—-with goods and services flowing from one country to another —-that it is hard to remember a time when managers and executives were only concerned about operations in their home country. But this world economy also requires a new set of communications rules and a whole new vocabulary when e-mails, faxes or phone calls can be filled with obscure or barely understood terms relating to both business and the legal environment in which one has to do business.

The *Dictionary of International Business Law* is designed to help operating managers deal with the basics of business and legal communication across borders. While never designed to be a true multicultural law reference, it does offer business people a clear and simple reference for the common words and acronyms used in the United States, the United Kingdom and the European Union. This is particularly important in the three areas of labor law, international finance and import/export. In every case definitions and examples are simple; they are meant to illustrate how a particular concept is used in actual practice.

Managers will find that the concise nature of the dictionary and cross referencing of the always difficult legal and business acronyms will be vital in their everyday pursuit of business.

Lucas Otto

A

AAL: Acronym in the United Kingdom for additional adoption leave, which is a period of 26 weeks of additional unpaid statutory leave directly added to ordinary adoption leave for any employee who has completed 26 weeks of continuous service at a firm.

ABA: *See* ***American Bar Association***.

Abandonment: Willingness, either implied or explicit, to give up a claim, title or even possession of property or a right.

Abeyance: A temporary suspension of ownership to a property, title or office before the correct owner is established.

ABI: Acronym for the Association of British Insurers, a trade association of about 40 insurance firms which transact about 95 percent of the insurance business in the U.K. It assists members with corporate governance issues.

Ability to Pay Theory: First appearing in English treatises on taxation, the principle states that the burden of taxation should be spread out on those who are able to pay. In recent theory, it is also called a progressive tax, meaning that as income and resources go up, so too, should the burden of taxation. If you make more, you pay more. On the other hand, if you make/own less, you pay less.

Abrogation: An agreement or contract that has been repealed or annulled. A country cancels certain rights given a company and the contract is now null and void. Overseas property or assets are expropriated or nationalized. For example over the years, oil and natural gas rights have been cancelled and the assets of the international companies have been seized. The former owners may be kept on to manage the newly nationalized company.

Absolute Leasehold Title: Generally considered to be the best form of title to registered land. This title vests in the proprietor the possession of the leasehold interest with all rights and privileges attached

Absolute Priority Rule: A fairly widely accepted concept internationally, the rule states that creditor's rights, especially secured creditors, are to be honored in full before stockholder's rights in liquidation or bankruptcy proceedings which are begun because an individual or a corporation is unable to meet their obligations.

Absolute Quota: A limit placed on the number of a particular product that can be imported; the absolute can be arbitrary or it can be a negotiated figure. In the United States, at various times, limits were place on imported cars by a general agreement between the government and international manufacturers. A time limit may be imposed where this quota is dropped. It is a form of protectionism, but not generally intended to be totally punitive as it is a temporary quota. A permanent quota would be illegal.

Absolute Title: Ownership of personal or real property that is unqualified, meaning that the owner, his or her heirs, representatives or assigns have absolute right to the property in question in perpetuity.

Abstract of Title: Generally relating to real estate, this is a complete, historical summary of all recorded documents relating to the property in question. As a rule, an abstract will summarize all recorded easements, mortgages, liens (including taxes), judgments and pending lawsuits that have a direct bearing on the title of the property.

Abuse of Process: Misuse of legal procedure. A frivolous or vexatious action. For example, issuing a claim which has already been decided by a competent court.

Abuses: A direct, intentional economic harm perpetrated by one company against another. The harm may be as simple as selling goods for resale at an inflated price or a systematic, limiting of competition through monopolistic practices.

ACAS: Acronym for Advisory Conciliation and Arbitration Service. Established under the Employment Protection Act 1975, the service was designed to support collective bargaining and work to improve employer/employee relations.

ACCA: *See **Association of Chartered Certified Accountants***

Accelerated Tariff Elimination: In an effort to promote international trade, two countries or a group of countries design an agreement to hasten the lowering of tariffs between and among the countries. The ultimate goal may be to eliminate all tariffs at some point in time.

Accelerated Receipt: A percentage reduction in the amount of compensation paid to an individual on termination of employment to reflect the fact that payment is received in one lump sum rather than over the whole notice period. The amount of the percentage reduction is commonly 50 percent in the United Kingdom, for example, of the current annual interest rate or half of the annual official court interest rate.

Acceleration Clause: A contractual or agreed provision that upon the occurrence of a stipulated act or event, a company's vested interest in a property will happen sooner than anticipated. An obligation owed to the company becomes immediately payable in full because of the debtor's nonpayment of an installment payment or some other violation of a provision of an agreement.

Acceptance: A contractual term that requires agreement to the provisos of either a verbal or written contact. As one of the three terms required for making a valid contract (the others being an offer and consideration), the offered terms do not make up a contract until the party to whom the contract is offered accepts the terms. Some forms of acceptance may be implied, but an offer in writing must be accepted in writing to constitute a valid acceptance.

Acceptance Credit: An arrangement with a commercial bank, often used in both the import and export businesses, as a means of financing transactions. This is often associated with a commercial letter of credit.

Acceptance Liability: The total liability that a bank assumes in accepting bills drawn on it by its customers, often used in conjunction with acceptance credit (*see above*) or letters of credit. The liability occurs in the event that the customer fails to deposit sufficient funds to match the acceptance credit.

Accepted Market Principle: For the purposes of the financial markets, a practice that is reasonably expected in one or more financial markets and is accepted by the competent authority. Such practices are a factor in deciding what is inside information in the commodity markets, for example, and provide a defense against the market abuse behavior of manipulating transactions where there is also a legitimate reason for the trading.

Accession: A principle by which an owner of a property is entitled to any additions to the property, whether these additions come naturally (the value of trees that grow on a property) or by the addition by someone's labor and effort (fixtures).

Accord and Satisfaction: A claim is settled by a creditor when the creditor agrees to accept in payment something different that anticipated. Two parties contract for goods or services, the first party complains that was what agreed to was not delivered. In order to avoid a lawsuit, the parties compromise, and a lesser amount is paid. Therefore, a new contract is made at a different rate and the accord and satisfaction are reached as each party gives up the right to sue.

***Accord d'Atypique*:** In France, a collective company agreement.

Accounting Standards Board: *See ASB*.

Accounts International Study Group (AISG): An attempt to smooth differences in international accounting theory and practice, the AISG was established for the purpose of publishing comparative studies on accounting issues in the United Kingdom, Canada and the United States.

Account Stated: Where a debtor is provided a hardcopy statement by a creditor detailing an amount owed as of a stated date. This hardcopy statement usually provides the debtor with the opportunity to pay the amount in whole or in part to the creditor.

Accord and Satisfaction: A claim is settled by a creditor when the creditor pays what is due.

Accrue: Where a debt continues to grow over time, such as by accumulating late fees or interest for nonpayment of a debt. Generally, anything can accrue, including time and legal rights to bring a lawsuit.

ACM: Acronym for the Arab Common Market, first begun in 1956 as the Arab Maghreb Union-a trade agreement seeking economic and political union among Algeria, Libya, Mauritania, Morocco and Tunisia. The ACM is basically inactive, despite several attempts to revive the trade agreement.

Acquiescence: A situation where an individual becomes legally bound, through either action or inaction, as a responsible party. In contractual situations, acceptance of a contract may be allowed even though an action taken by an individual was not meant as a straightforward acceptance of a contract, because that action may imply acknowledgment of the contract. Inaction may occur where a party knows it could bring legal action, but lets a great deal of time pass-raising the implication that waiver of these rights to legal action may have occurred.

Acquisitions: In a business context, the taking over of one company by another. The acquisition may be by mutual consent or it may be hostile, e.g. an effort to gain a majority control without management's consent or agreement. In almost all major economies, acquisitions are closely monitored and regulated by such bodies as the European Union.

Acquisitions Agreement: Known as the sale and purchase agreement or as a share/asset purchase agreement. This document contains the terms of the deal, including price, payment and conditions for completing the deal.

Across the Board: All members of a group, class or association. Taxes may be reduced across the board, meaning for all groups of classifications of tax payers. Further, all employees will receive a pay increase of four percent, across the board, regardless of level or length of service

Act: The process by which a legislative bill, after going through several stages, becomes a law.

Acting in Concert: A group acting together in a takeover situation. Persons acting in concert are those who cooperate to obtain or consolidate control of a company (or to prevent others from making an offer for the company). Control in this context often means 30 percent of the voting rights in the target company. The percentage for control can vary from one jurisdiction to another.

Action: French equivalent for shares or stock in a company; action ordinaire is common stock.

Act of God: An occurrence, such as a tsunami, earthquake, tornado or natural death, brought about by natural causes or nature and absent human interference. These types of occurrences may provide a legal defense to contracted parties for duties which are incomplete, as well as for physical and property damage caused by the occurrence.

Act of State Doctrine: In international law, the fact that each country has its own control of what takes place within its territory.

ADA: *See **Americans with Disabilities Act**.*

ADB: Acronym for the Arab Development Bank or the Asian Development Bank, both of which were founded with the intention of facilitating trade and economic reforms in their respective regions.

Addendum: Where a document is added or attached to another document as an accompanying piece to form the complete document.

Additional Adoptive Leave: *See AAL.*

ADEA: *See **Age Discrimination in Employment Act**.*

Adhesion Contract: Usually a form contract, this preprinted document provides no opportunity for collaboration of its terms, and these terms are usually heavily one sided and to the advantage of the individual providing the contract. An example of this kind of contract is a lease presented by the landlord for signature by a future tenant.

Ad Hoc Arbitration: Where the procedure is determined independently by the parties and the arbitrators, without the involvement of an arbitral institution. Questions such as costs and procedure are decided by the parties, and failing agreement between them, by the arbitrators.

Adjudication: A hybrid procedure which usually provides for the adjudicator's decision to be binding, but only for an interim period until completion of a project or until review in or court proceedings. It is best known in the construction field where the Housing Grants, Construction and Regeneration Act 1996 in the United Kingdom requires all construction contracts entered into after 1 May 1998 to provide for rapid adjudication of all disputes.

Adjustable Peg: A system of fixed, locked exchange rates that is set by the governments directly involved or by multi-governmental agreement in the international currency exchange markets. These rates may be modified, however, when a participating nation has a highly unfavorable experience as its currency no longer reflects economic reality.

Adjustment Approach: In the matter of reducing balance of payments, efforts made by governments may include: monetary modifications, currency exchange rate changes, new tariff regulations and government interaction in the currency or interest rate markets.

Adjustment Bonds: In corporate reorganizations, existing debt is consolidated into one class of debt (bond) with a uniform interest rate. Interest is payable only if earned, that is only if the company has sufficient earnings to pay the interest, after all other senior fixed income obligations have been paid. Adjustment bonds are sometimes called income bonds.

Administor ad Colligendum: An individual or entity selected by a court or to handle the proceeds received from selling foreign assets.

Administrative Law: A general term describing the powers and operations of governmental regulatory agencies to control excesses in the financial, banking and general business markets. Administrative law sets a series of checks and balances; for example, antitrust or restraint of trade legislation that most sophisticated economies use to govern monopolies and protect the consumer.

Admission: An acknowledgement of the truth of a fact or allegation. Admissions are made by or on behalf of a party to a dispute before or during proceedings. They can be made in various forms, in writing or orally, informally and formally.

ADR: *See* ***alternative dispute resolution***; *also* **American depository receipts**.

Ad Valorem: Literally according to value, the term is usually used in the context of levying taxes on imports. There are two ways to calculate duties: one is by weight or number of units and the other is the declared value of the goods being imported.

***Ad Valorem* Duty:** A duty levied as a proportion of the price or value of an imported commodity.

Advance: A portion of money prepaid with the expectation of services, with a final or full payment to occur when services are completed. An example would be an author advanced a portion of money with a final installment paid upon completion of a book.

Adversary System: Typical in common law countries, whereby advocates present their case in litigation before a neutral judge. In continental

Europe, the inquisitorial system is used whereby a judge or group of judges investigates the case.

Adverse Possession: Where one who is without legal title to land becomes the recognized legal owner of the land due to the fact that he or she resided on the land for a sufficient amount of time to acquire the land as their own. The time period to acquire legal title of land by adverse possession varies, and in some places adverse possession of land is prohibited.

Advisory Capacity: A consultant or advisor lacks authority to make substantive changes or adjustments in an agreement without the approval of those in authority. For example, an IT consultant, acting in an advisory capacity, would not have the authority to change a purchase order without the express permission of the company's officers.

Advisory Conciliation and Arbitration Service: *See* ACAS.

AESOP: Acronym for All Employee Ownership Share Plan in the United Kingdom. Similar plans are available in the United States and most advanced economic countries.

AFDB: Acronym for the African Development Bank which was founded in 1964 with the intention to promote economic and social development throughout Africa. Its 77 members are from Africa, America and Europe and are particularly concerned with alleviating debt in Africa.

Affidavit: A document or statement wherein the person, before signing, swears under oath that the contents within the document are true and accurate, to the best of his knowledge. This written statement is often used in court in place of the testimony of the witness who signed it. The individual giving the oath, either a notary or other officer allowed to administer the oath, will also sign the document attesting that the oath was given.

Affiliate: A partly or fully owned unit of a larger company. Affiliates include a wholly owned branch, foreign-incorporated subsidiary and joint ventures, for example.

Affiliation Privilege: Favorable European tax regime or treatment between a parent company and its subsidiary in the context of the payment of dividends.

Affirmative Action: The act of providing preferential hiring, admission or advancement opportunities to cultural and racial minorities in an attempt to help remedy past discriminatory workplace and educational practices. Businesses, governmental agencies and educational institutions have utilized this practice. Courts have ruled against some forms of affirmative action, stating that there can be a presence of reverse discrimination such as in hiring and college admissions.

Affirmative Dumping Decision: A deliberate decision to allow an industry to sell products below their normal selling price in a foreign country. For example, in an effort to protect domestic steel production, a country allows the selling of steel below international prices. These kinds of dumping decisions are arbitrated by the international courts and are the cause of a good deal of friction among countries and regions.

Affreightment: A contractual agreement between a company and carrier to ship products overseas or domestically.

Afloat: In maritime trade, a reference to the fact that goods have not reached their destination and are still in the process of being transported by sea. Goods that have arrived and have not been unloaded are not deemed to be afloat.

African Development Bank: *See* AFDB.

Age Discrimination: When an employer hires, terminates or lays-off an individual between ages 40 to 70 years (U.S.) and disparate treatment of this current or potential employee is proven by a claimant, then the actions taken by the employer may be considered illegal under the Age Discrimination in Employment Act (ADEA).

Age Discrimination in Employment Act (ADEA): Federal law prohibiting employment decision discrimination of workers older than 40 years of age- principally those decisions regarding termination and which employees might be laid off.

Agency for International Development: *See* AID.

Agent: A person granted the authority by another (this other person is usually referred to as the principal) to act on behalf and for the benefit of this other person when dealing with third parties. The agent's authority usually allows him/her to bind a principal to agreements with third parties as if the principal made the decisions himself-this authority given to an agent may also bind a principal to potential liability issues.

Agent de Change: Title given to a member of the Paris Bourse; used in other European stock markets as well.

Agent for Acceptance of Service: This individual is named and authorized by a corporation (usually within the articles of incorporation or by other analogous documents filed with the governing authories) to accept service of claims against the corporation, as well as service of lawsuits. A professional agent that represents several corporations is often designated for this position by larger corporations that have operations in several states.

Aggravated Damages: Damages offered for mental distress or injury to feelings caused by the manner with which a wrong was committed by the defendant.

Aggregate Limit of Liability: In the United States, the maximum an insurance company will cover an insured in a given period of time (e.g., a year, a lifetime, etc,) regardless of the number of claims submitted to the insurance company during that period. The limit is clearly delineated in the insurance policy and is either predetermined by company policy or is determined by negotiations between the insurance company and the insured.

For example, health care insurers might offer a $5 million life-time limit on what they will pay for medical expenses for one individual insured or his entire family, depending on the policy and the premiums.

AGIO: In Continental Europe, this is the premium of metallic currency over other, legal tender such as paper money.

AGM: Acronym for annual general meeting, which includes shareholders and directors at least every 15 months. While the Companies Act of 1985 does not specify the actual agenda of the meeting, generally directors are elected (or re-elected), review of the annual accounts and compensation of the auditors, among other issues, are taken up. There must be 21 clear days notice announcing the meeting. Most U.S. companies, including all public ones, are also required to have an annual meeting.

Agreement: Where two or more parties have a meeting of the minds concerning a set of duties, responsibilities and rights in regards to a particular issue. Although in contractual terms an agreement can also mean contract, one can have an agreement without legal obligation.

Agricultural Marketing Service (AMS): A service of the United States government to assure foreign purchasers of United States goods that they satisfy quality standards and contractual commitments.

AID: Acronym for Agency for International Development, sometimes referred to as USAID. As an agency of the U. S. Government, it is responsible for much of the non-military aid granted to other nations. It addition to economic aid, it also dispenses humanitarian aid in times of national crisis, famine or natural disasters.

AIM Rules for Companies: Acronym for alternative investment market. Published by the London Stock Exchange (LSE) the AIM rules set out the rules and responsibilities for companies admitted to AIM.

Air Pocket: This is a stock market expression indicating that the shares have suffered a sharp and abrupt weakness in the value of the shares.

The decline is generally out of proportion in regards to the value of the shares. Often it is caused by more sell orders than buy orders.

AISG: *See* ***Accountants International Study Group***.

Ajr: Under Islamic law and tradition, this is a commission paid; or a fee charged for various services.

Aleatory: Means uncertain, and this term often can be found in insurance contracts where payment is reliant on the happening of a contingent event to an insured.

Alien: Any individual residing in a country but who is not a citizen of that country. Depending upon their status, they may engage in business, write contracts and take employment, as well as pay taxes. Illegal aliens in theory have none of these rights.

All Employee Share Option Plan: *See* AESOP.

Allonge: Where a piece of paper is attached to a negotiable instrument (like a check or contract) to allow for more signatures, because there is not enough space on the negotiable instrument.

All or None: An investment banker chooses to underwrite all of a company's securities, preferring not to participate with other investment banks in the underwriting. Alternatively, an investor may execute an all or none order in which his broker is directed to either purchase or sell an order of securities totally or none at all.

Alpha Stock: The London Stock Exchange (LSE) classifies shares by how frequently they were dealt (traded); typically, these companies are the largest or blue chip stocks. Beta and gamma shares are typically smaller companies, less actively traded. This system has been replaced with the normal market size (NMS) classification system.

Alteration: Any changes which alters the contract of any party to a negotiable instrument in any respect whatsoever.

Alter Ego: Where a business entity or organization is developed for the sole purpose of providing the person that has actual control over the operation with a legal shield. *See* ***piercing the veil*** as a connected term.

Alternative Dispute Resolution (ADR): A process whereby an appointed third party helps to resolve the disputes of other parties, rather than those parties having to go through the litigation process of the court system. This is a private action and usually is in the form of a mediation or arbitration.

Alternative Investment Market: *See* AIM.

Amalgamation: To combine or merge two things together to form one single entity; like the combining of two companies to form one under the same name.

Amanah: In Islamic tradition, the word generally means trustworthiness, reliability or honesty. In the area of law or business, it can mean deposits in trusts or holding property in trust in a fiduciary manner.

Ambulatory: A term that may be used when dealing with written documents; it means it is not written in stone, so it can be altered, revoked or changed.

American Bar Association: Established in 1878, the association of lawyers is one of the largest in the world. Its stated goal is to promote the improvement and practice of law, including setting standards for prospective lawyers. Generally, it promotes awareness of the legal system and the advancement of professional standards among its members. Not all American lawyers are members of the ABA

American Depository Receipt (ADR): These are receipts that are provided by United States banks to citizens of the United States in substitution of ownership of foreign stock shares. These ADRs help U.S. citizens avoid having to trade the actual foreign shares, as they can be traded within U.S. stock exchanges.

American Selling Price (ASP): The price used for customs purposes, as a tax base for determining import duties. Under this system, the domestic price of competing goods in the United States is used for this purpose. Since this price is commonly above the actual foreign price, this system is often construed as a protectionist device.

Americans with Disabilities Act (ADA): A federal law which prohibits discrimination against people with disabilities in employment, public services and places accommodating the public. Similar legislation exists in the United Kingdom and the rest of the European Union.

AMF: Acronym for the Arab Monetary Fund, which was founded in 1976 and whose main goal is to encourage the creation and development of Arab financial markets and, generally, the promotion of trade.

Amortization: Where a debt is paid by setting up a recurrent payment plan that includes payment of interest on the debt along with some of the principal in each payment. This process is usually formulated through the use of recognized mathematical formulas, and it is often used on land-property loans and automobile or other large financed items.

AMS: *See* ***Agricultural Marketing Service***.

ANCOM: Acronym for the Andean Common Market, now more commonly called the Andean Community of Nations, consisting of

Bolivia, Columbia, Ecuador, Peru and Venezuela. While membership continues to change as countries are added or are dropped, the overall goal is a common market for economic development.

Andean Common Market: *See* ANCOM.

Animus Contrahendi: With intent to contract.

Annual General Meeting: *See* AGM.

Annual Information Update: The Prospectus Rules requires that all listed companies prepare a document on an annual basis which contains all regulated information that the company has published or made available within and outside of the E.U. within the last 12 months.

Annual Meeting: Used often in businesses and corporations to denote a meeting of directors or corporate shareholders. A directorial meeting is usually done for consideration purposes, such as to discuss and consider large purchases for the corporation, whereas a shareholders' meeting usually takes place with an agenda designed primarily to either vote on substantial changes to a corporation (for example, a merger) or to elect directors.

Annuity: Usually denotes a policy (annuity policy) that is purchased with the prospect of paying its purchaser dividends possibly over his lifetime, or on a regular basis over several years.

Antecedents: In the course of business or pending a legal contract, a credit history is obtained. Parties to an agreement have the right to know the business history of one or all parties to an agreement. The overall goal is to establish that the company is a stable, on-going concern and has the ability to fulfill its obligations in business dealings.

Anticipatory Breach: Where the obligations of one individual to a contract are not met, because that individual repudiated his or her obligations to the contract prior to carrying-out his or her contract duties. Although an individual can repudiate by verbalization or by action, once repudiation occurs the other party to the deal will be released from contract duties.

Antitrust Laws: While the term is in common use in the United States, other countries use the term competition law. No matter how used, most major economies have laws preventing anti-competitive business practices (monopolies) and unfair business practices. Competition laws make practices illegal that hurt consumers or other businesses unfairly. European Union laws date back to the Treaty of Rome; Australia functions under the Trade Practices Act and in the United States, a variety of laws, based on the Sherman Antitrust Act and the Clayton Act, govern antitrust activities.

Anton Piller Order: Search and seizure orders by which a court provides for the preservation of documents and articles relating to a claim.

Apparent Authority: A situation where an individual is cloaked with the appearance of being the agent of either an employer or principal, and is represented to a third party as having the power to act on the behalf of an employer or principal, and thus binding the principal to the agent's dealings and acts (i.e. contracts). The mere appearance of authority of an agent, when relied upon by a third party to a deal, will often bind the principal to that deal under agency law.

Application: An offer to buy or to enter into some kind of contract. Applications may be made for business loans, relief from a court, a mortgage or even for letters of credit. Because it is merely an offer, it does not bind either party; there must be an acceptance for the transaction to be legal and binding.

Apportionment: A process by which something is split up and dispersed into balanced parts. If a contract is apportioned each party would only have to perform his or her end of the contract equal to that of the other individual(s) of the contract.

Appraise: The process by which a professional, usually an appraiser, assesses the value, or loss of value, of both real and personal property (i.e. real estate, paintings, etc.). This estimation is often done due to a court order in various legal proceedings when a fair market value is needed on property; it is also used in business settings (business valuation for taxes or a sale) and when private individuals desire a value on property.

Appreciation: Where property, real or personal, increases in value over time without having to improve the property for the growth to occur. Often appreciation is a result of inflation or an increasing scarcity for a particular asset. Location of property, say in the center city, many cause it to appreciate out of proportion to other properties in an area.

Approved Executive Share Option Scheme: In the United Kingdom, the directors of a firm can decide which directors shall personally benefit from the plan. An individual is given an option for a specific number of shares and a date before which they cannot be exercised. Exercise cannot be more than 10 years after the grant of option.

Approved Scheme: A share scheme in the United Kingdom approved by HM Revenue & Customs which enjoys valuable tax benefits.

Appurtenance: Means something, a right or a restriction, that attaches to and goes with a piece of real property. Illustrations of this often are used in real property law, and an example is where one party, possibly a neighbor, is granted a right of way over an individual's property. These rights go with the property.

Arab Common Market: *See* ACM.

Arab Monetary Fund: *See* AMF.

Arbeitsamt: Local German labor office to which redundancies are reported.

Arbitrage: Assuming that prices are not efficient in one market versus another, arbitrage is the process of buying-stocks, currency, gold or silver-in one market and selling it for a profit (spread) in another. Because of increasingly rapid communication through worldwide technology, arbitrage is far more difficult to accomplish consistently.

Arbitration: A process where parties to a dispute meet with a neutral third party or a panel in an attempt to avoid the processes of court. This neutral third party or a panel then listens to presented evidence by both sides and renders a decision based on the merits of the parties' arguments. This decision and award, often handed down by an arbitrator, is final and binding on all parties.

Arbitrator: This is usually the individual that presides over the arbitration process and is the person that renders the final, binding decision based on the evidence presented. Although often an attorney, he does not have to be, and can be an expert in a specific discipline.

Area Development Agreement: A franchisor requires a franchisee to operate within a specific geographic area and it further restrains the franchisee from sub-franchising to a third party.

Arm's Length: A term used when two parties, without restraint and in which each party is independent of the other, form an agreement. If a relationship was previously formed that provides one party with the power to control an agreement over the other, this deal probably was not made at arms' length.

Arrears: A situation where a debt, which is due, goes unpaid. This unpaid amount often accumulates over time (an example is when rent goes unpaid).

Arrestment: Similar to a garnishment, in Scottish law it is an order to freeze assets, a sum of money for example, held by someone in debt for the benefit of the defender.

Article 81: The overall intent of this article from the E.C. treaty is to prohibit anticompetitive actions, agreements or practices which may affect trade and which have as their object the restriction of competition within the common market.

Article 82: An article of the E.C. treaty, its purpose is to prohibit any firm with a dominant position within the common market from exploiting that dominance within the common market.

Articles of Association: Often known simply as the articles, one of the basic documents of a company which sets out the management and administrative structure of the firm. Most of the internal affairs of the company are regulated through these documents, including the issuing of shares, board and shareholder meetings, the duties of the directors, dividend policy and the ability to borrow in order to finance the company. (*See* ***articles of incorporation bellow***).

Articles of Incorporation: A principal document (a charter) of a corporation that puts forth the name of the corporation, purpose of the business, types of stock that can be issued, the amount of stock to be issued, the directors, etc. This charter often is restricted by state rules, as each state has its own approval system regarding articles-which includes requirements and regulations for issuing shares. In the U. S. the Secretary of State of a specific state often is where articles of incorporation are filed and approved.

ASB: Acronym for Accounting Standards Board which issues accounting standards in the form of Financial Reporting Standards (FRSs) and has promulgated rules for standards in the form of Statements of Standard Accounting Practice (SSAP).

Asian Development Bank: *See* ***ADB***.

As Is: This term is often used in a contract for the sale of goods, in which the property being purchased is sold free and clear by the seller, in the condition it is currently at the time of sale. The buyer in turn agrees to take the property, effectively waiving any right after taking possession concerning the property's condition-even if it turns out to be defective or faulty. Before taking possession of the property the buyer must be allowed to inspect it, and the seller, if found to have knowingly concealed a defect, could potentially cause the contract to be cancelled.

ASP: *See* ***American selling price***.

Assess: Where a property is appointed a fixed value, often with the intention of computing real property taxes or for the purposes of selling the property or for a settlement of an estate.

Asset(s): Property that has monetary and sometimes sentimental value. These items are often found in businesses, and usually can be found in business balance sheets in the forms of fixed assets, current assets and business goodwill.

Asset-Based Financing: Pools of debt from credit cards, mortgages, student loans and trade receivables are packaged and sold to investors as asset-back securities. The resulting sales provides liquidity that then allows issuing institutions such as banks to write more mortgages or make additional loans to businesses. Investors, particularly pension schemes, buy the resulting securities as part of their investment portfolio. These asset-backed securities are bought and sold on international markets just as stocks and bonds are. Individual investors rarely participate as the resulting asset-backed securities are denominated in huge sums.

Assign: A process by which real property or a right is given or transferred to another; the person receiving this property or right is often referred to as the assignee.

Assignats: Issued in 1789 by the provisional French government, this was paper money backed by the seized assets and estates of the nobility during and after the French Revolutionary War. In the end, so much was printed that it eventually became valueless.

Assignment: The actual act of giving or transferring an interest in a property or right by one person to another. This process is often used when dealing with real property

Assignment for Benefit of Creditors: A process by which a debtor has a trustee and through a payment schedule, pays the debtor's debt with a portion of the debtor's income.

Assists: American manufactured component parts that are shipped to foreign manufacturing plants for incorporation into products that are assembled there and subsequently exported back to the United States. A duty may be assessed on these components when they are imported back as part of the completed finished goods.

Association: Where a group of people, for either social or business-related activities, come together because they have a common interest in what the group is doing. This is not considered a corporation or partnership, although it can be structured with formal rules and guidelines.

Association of British Insurers: *See ABI*.

Association of Chartered Certified Accountants (ACCA): An accounting society in the United Kingdom (chartered under the royal seal) whose members work in both the public and the private sector; members must hold a practicing certificate, be insured against liability and have a practice that is open for public scrutiny (if working for the public sector).

Assumption of Risk: Often a defense to a negligence claim, this is a situation where an individual purposely puts himself in an obviously dangerous, or potentially dangerous situation, and comes away injured (for example, rock climbing). The individual should have recognized the obvious danger, but chose to go ahead with the activity, essentially assuming the risk. The can also be applied to contract law.

Assurance: A term interchangeable with insurance but used in connection with life insurance business, as assurance implies the certainty of an event and insurance the probability of something happening.

Assured: A title given to a person or an entity that is insured.

At Risk: A tax concept (United States) that limits the deductibility of losses from business and income-producing activities. At risk limits apply to individuals and closely-held corporations and were established to prevent the deductibility of losses in excess of the actual amount of the investment that was made.

Attachment: A term often used in cases when money is owed, where a party to a case (usually the plaintiff) seeks to seize the money or property of the party they are bringing suit against before a judgment is rendered in the case-under the assumption that the plaintiff will eventually win at trial. This basically provides a security to the plaintiff, because that money or property will cover the eventual judgment. A hearing before a judge is required before this process can take place in order to allow both sides the opportunity to argue their positions as it relates to the danger that the individual being sued will either not be present for the trial or will be unable when the trial concludes to make the necessary payment upon final judgment. A bond must be required of the plaintiff by the judge to ensure potential damages to the individual are paid if the attachment does not prove to have been needed.

Attest: A process by which a document is corroborated as authentic (usually done by an individual or individuals, and it is often done in writing). This term can also be used where one observes and confirms that another signed a document in their presence.

Attorney: In the United States, this is a person authorized and licensed to practice law by the highest court of a state or jurisdiction, and acts as an agent who is authorized to work on behalf of another in a legal capacity. In the U.S., attorneys perform both in court and out of court pleadings, where as in the United Kingdom this process is split between barristers (who try cases in court) and solicitors (who perform legal tasks, but not in court).

Attorney's Fee: The payment by a client for legal representation and services.

Attorney's Work Product: These are documents prepared by an attorney in preparation of a case for a client, and can encompass written documents, notes, charts, conversational materials that have been transcribed into written format, as well as other documents used to help prepare for a case. These are documents that do not have to be introduced in court or provided to opposing counsel, as they are created merely for the preparation of a case.

Attornment: Where a party gives his or her permission, either implicitly or explicitly, to the transfer of a right to another. This term can often be found in tenancy law, when a property owner sells the property to another and the tenant that lived on the property before it was sold consents to being a tenant of the new owner/landlord.

Attractive Nuisance Doctrine: Where something is left on a piece of property (like construction equipment) or a property is left in a certain condition which would be both attractive and unsafe for children curiously entering that property; the result is to make the person that left the property in that condition negligent for potential injuries to the children.

At Will Employment: A term relating to the employment status of an individual (and found in employment contracts) that designates that the employee works at the will of the employer. It allows an employer to avoid termination claims, because it puts the burden on the terminated employee to show a belief that he or she was a permanent employee.

Atypical Worker: A worker who does not fall into the usual employment categories, for example one who works at home, who works part time or works flexible hours. These kinds of workers are increasingly being recognized in recent legislation, including Fixed Term Employees Regulations in 2002.

Auction: An open market in which there is one seller but many possible buyers. While there are multiple versions of the basic theme, buyers complete against each other, making successive bids, until a final price is reached-thus the highest bidder. Typically, auctions are used to sell excess inventory or real property for which there has been little market or interest.

Audit: A process by which the financial records of a business, person or other entity are examined by a trained and certified accountant. The accountant will or may log improper or thoughtless practices, make certain recommendations to help make future improvements in the business and balance the financial books.

Autarchy: A term of German origin, it basically refers to economic self-sufficiency. A nation reaches autarchy when it manages to provide for as much of its domestic needs through it own natural resources, technology, labor, farm production and financial resources. An ideal position during war, it is an impossible concept in the contemporary economic world where trade and international finance are so prominent.

Authority: Often used in business where one gives another the power to act on their behalf, or to order others to act (i.e., principal to agent, employer to employee, corporation to its officers). The various types of authorities are: apparent authority, expressed authority, limited authority, implied authority and general authority.

Authorized Payment: Any payment by a registered pension scheme that is permitted by the Finance Act of 2004; all others are considered unauthorized.

Automatically Unfair Dismissal: In the United Kingdom, certain dismissals are automatically unfair-for example, when statutory dismissal and disciplinary procedures are not followed, because of trade union membership, pregnancy or maternity.

Aval: A third party agreement to guarantee payment on a promissory note, for example; avals are not fully recognized under English law but are used frequently in the E. U.

***Avoir Fiscal*:** A tax credit, under the French system, which is granted automatically to a recipient of a paid dividend. The reduction of taxes can range from 10 percent to 50 percent of the value of the net dividend.

Avulsion: A term used mainly in property law, it is a sudden change in the natural course of a stream or river, and the border of two properties-which were defined by the waterway's channel-are changed by the altered course.

Award: When a party to a judicial proceeding, arbitration or administrative claim is given money following a judgment in his or her favor.

Away: Quoted price differing from the prevailing market price for a particular product or service.

B

B2B: Acronym for business to business transaction.

B2C: Acronym for business to consumer transaction.

Backdating: Placing a date on a document or check prior to the time it was actually prepared (and then so should have been dated). In most cases, backdating is illegal. Recent scandals have been uncovered with large corporations concerning the backdating of options for key employees, for example.

Back to Back: Typically, a loan is made in one nation in its currency against a loan in another nation in another currency.

Back-to-Back Loans: Two affiliates of the same company are located in different countries and borrow each other's currency for a stated period of time with an agreed upon repayment schedule and amount. These are sometimes called link financing or fronting loans and solve the problem of high interest rates or not very sophisticated currency markets in one of the countries.

Backwardation: The practice of delaying settlement on the London Stock Exchange. An investor wishes to postpone delivery of shares, with the belief that the share price will fall and he can deliver cheaper shares to the buyer. The buyer will agree to this arrangement if some additional premium is offered to compensate the buyer.

Bad Debt: When a debt is owed but it is unrealistic that it can be collected. This uncollectible debt often results from bankruptcy or when the debt has gone unmanaged over a period of time

Bad Faith: Meaning to intend to deceive by performing an intentional dishonest act to acquire an advantage in contract obligations; to mislead another or to gain entrance into an agreement without the intention or means to fulfill it.

Bai al Arboon: Under Islamic law or tradition, this is a sale secured by a deposit; a security deposit is provided before the sale and the security deposit is forfeited if the buyer does not keep his end of the agreement.

Bai al Inah: An individual sells an asset to a financial institution and then buys it back at a higher price; a sale and buy-back transaction.

Bailee: When temporary control or custody of another's property is held by a third party.

Bailment: Possession and control of property or assets are transferred to a third party for some specific purpose. The third party does not have title to the goods. For example it is held in trust and once the transaction has taken place, the property is returned to the owner.

Bai Bithman Ajil: Under Islamic practice, the bank buys goods for a client who then holds and sells the goods to the client with the appropriate markup over time; in effect an installment payment plan.

Bai Dayn: Under Islamic law, simple debt financing of a short term nature (year or less); these are the only short-term debts that can be traded.

Bai Isitijrar: In Islamic tradition, a simple agreement to deliver goods or services to a client at an agreed about quantity on a regular basis for an agreed upon price.

Bai Salam: The financial institution pays in advance for a specific asset which the seller will supply on a pre-agreed date or a forward-financing transaction-completed under Islamic law.

Bai Wafa: Simply a sale and buy-back agreement, where the seller and buyer agree on the purchase under Islamic tradition.

Bait and switch: A deceitful tactic used in sales to lure people to a business with the promise of a low cost item, only to inform a customer once in the business establishment that the item is no longer available or is inferior in quality. The seller then attempts to switch the customer in the direction of a more expensive item. This tactic is often seen in retail businesses, but has also been documented in financial services businesses as well.

Balance Due: Where an account still has an amount owed on a debt or the amount of principal still owed on a promissory note. The balance due on promissory notes is not the sums of the leftover installments-since these installments include interest payments-but rather it may be the principal due without further interest.

Balance of Payments: A theoretical and complex set of financial relationships whereby a record of all of a country's international exchange of good and services, IOUs, financial assets and investments should be in balance between one country and another. In reality, many countries import more than they export, so the balance of payments is not the theoretical zero.

Balance Sheet: Often prepared each month, quarter, annually or at the sale of a business, it is a statement that lays out the overall condition of a business by detailing the financial status of its liabilities and assets at particular period of time. This is not the same as a profit and loss statement.

Bank Discount Rate: A means of calculating loan interest based on the amount to be repaid. The net proceeds of the loan, that is usable money by the lender, is less the stated discount (interest rate). Assume $5,000 borrowed and the cost of the loan is $900, the net to the borrower is $4,100 but the full $5,000 must be repaid in the end of the loan.

Bank Guarantee: Covering a risk or obligation on a transaction by guaranteeing payment, perhaps based on some larger line of credit or some pre-existing collateral, or assistance offered by a third party.

Bank Holiday: Scheduled, specific dates when banks are closed in England, Scotland, Wales, Northern Ireland and Ireland. These are generally business holidays as well and the times and dates vary by district and custom.

Banking Support: When banks purchase large enough numbers of securities to stabilize the financial markets. This is a largely forgotten function of a bank, as any intervention in the capital markets usually comes from institutional buyers/sellers or by governments themselves.

Bank of England: The central banking institution of the United Kingdom, commonly called the Old Lady of Threadneedle Street. The bank was first chartered in 1694 and its regulation and function have continually been amended by acts of Parliament since then. Like most central banks, its role is to keep order and liquidity in the banking system and to coordinate its functions with other central banks.

Bank of France: Established in 1800 at a time when no other French bank existed, the Bank of France was the largest commercial bank in France until recent memory-serving the public directly. It no longer serves as a primary commercial bank.

Bank of International Settlements: *See BIS*.

Bank Rate: Typically referred to as the prime rate, it represents the lowest interest rate charged to other banks. It is the determinant of what commercial and savings banks will charge businesses and consumers. Tightening (raising) the bank rate is a typical way for a central bank to control inflation and slow the economy; the reverse is also true-lower the rate to stimulate borrowing and business activity.

Bankruptcy: A condition where proceedings are held under federal law allowing an insolvent individual or entity (debtors) to discharge debts and/or get protection from creditors while trying to repay them. In the United States, Chapter 7 bankruptcy is a liquidation bankruptcy, and involves discharging debts by surrendering assets, whereas, Chapter 13 allows the individual or entity to provide the court with a plan for repaying the debt. Chapter 11 bankruptcy (reorganization) is reserved for businesses and individuals with extremely large debts.

Bankruptcy Court: When an issue arises under the Federal Bankruptcy Act, these are the federal courts that deal with and preside over bankruptcy matters.

Bargain: Where two parties, in exchange of consideration, mutually and voluntarily agree to a deal or contract. Consideration can take the form of goods, money, services or mutual promises.

Bargaining Unit: A union, or other organization, representing employees in negotiations with an employer or group of employers on wages, working conditions, benefits, pensions and other matters.

BARNEEC: Acronym for best available techniques not entailing excessive cost. Frequently a requirement under U.K. law to protect the environment, for example, by eliminating emissions into the air.

Barratry: Damage or fraud committed against a ship or its cargo by the captain or the ship's crew which would result in loss to the owner of the ship or the owner of the cargo. It is not a risk covered by the carrier, but must be insured by some kind of marine insurance specific to barratry.

Barriers to Entry: Obstacles to prevent new companies from entering a business or industry; such barriers may be legal, but can easily be interpreted as unfair competition. The high cost of building an oil refinery may be a barrier to entry, but that does not make it illegal.

Barrister: In the United Kingdom, under the two-tier bar system, these are the legal advocates who try cases in court, as opposed to solicitors who perform legal tasks, but not in court. In the United States this is also a formal reference for a lawyer or attorney; although in the U.S. an attorney can perform both in court and out of court legal tasks.

Barter: The legal transfer of property or commodities without the use of money. Barter was one of the oldest means of exchange in mercantile society. A measure of salt is exchanged for a bushel of wheat, for example.

Basel Accord: Developed in 1988 by the Basel Committee on Banking Supervision, the accord's goal was to achieve international agreement on capital adequacy requirements of banks and to establish minimal capital standards for all banks.

Basic State Pension (BSP): The primary pension scheme in the United Kingdom for individuals who have reached state pension age. Category A BSP is paid to individuals with a full record of National Insurance contributions; Category B BSP is designed for a widow or widower or surviving civil partners not eligible for Category A BSP.

Basis: The rate of yield to maturity on bonds and other debt instruments. It can also be the spread between the spot price of a commodity and the futures contract price.

Bearer: The person holding a negotiable instrument, such as a check, bank draft, promissory note or bond. The holder of this negotiable instrument can be anyone, and if the document reads payable to bearer, then it can be negotiated by whoever holds the document and that person can receive the funds due on it.

Bearer Paper: The negotiable instrument (i.e. a check, bank draft, bond, etc.) that can be negotiated by whoever possesses it.

Beneficial Interest: Where a party has a right to some profit, distribution or benefit from a trust or contract. This interest is different from those of a trustee.

Benefit: When dealing in contractual law, this term designates any profit, privilege or acquired right gained through a contract; whereas, when dealing with worker's compensation it refers to an insurance payment resulting from an on-the-job fatal accident (non-fatal accidents receive compensation).

Benefit Principle of Taxation: As opposed to the ability-to-pay principle, this theory of taxation says that those who receive the benefits of the public good should finance said public good. If you benefit from a bridge being built, you should be taxed for the bridge.

Berne Convention: Created in Berne, Switzerland in 1886 (it has been revised) and called the Convention for the Protection of Literary and Artistic Works, this international copyright treaty serves to standardize copyright protection among its signing countries.

Berth Terms: Loading and discharging fees are the responsibility of a ship's owner.

Bespoke: A computer program or an entire computer system that is custom-made to a client's specifications.

Best Available Techniques Not Entailing Excessive Cost: *See* BARNEEC.

Best Efforts: When underwriting and selling a security, the investment bank makes a commitment to the company to do its best to sell the securities to the public at the best price the market will bear.

Best Evidence Rule: A legal rule stipulating that an original document or piece of evidence is superior to a copy, and if an original document exists and can be produced, a copy will not be allowed in a trial.

***Betriebsvereinabarung*:** Collective bargaining agreement in Germany.

Betterment: The value of property increases or decreases as a result of an action or proposed action by a public body-adding new sewers and roads might increase values but building a public dump nearby may decrease values.

Betterments: Two parties contract for the building of a home; an improvement better than specified in the contract is substituted-brick walls instead of wooden walls.

BFP: Acronym meaning bona fide purchaser. *See* ***bona fide purchaser*** for a full definition of this term.

Bid: An offer to purchase something or to perform a particular service at a competitive price. In auctions this term relates to offers to purchase by bidders at the highest price, whereas contractors make bids, often in competition with other contractors' competitive offers, to work on specific projects, with the lowest offer often getting the work.

Bid-rigging: Prohibited by law, two or more companies conspire to fix bids at similar prices or agree ahead of time which companies will bid on a public project.

Bifurcation: A situation where a judge, before a trial is to begin, divides issues so that one issue can be ruled upon before arguments begin on another issue.

Big Bang: The reforms and liberalization of the rules and regulations of the London capital markets in 1986.

Bilateral Contract: A situation where parties come to an agreement, through the exchange of promises, to do something for the other in the future.

Bilateral Monopoly: A marketplace with only one buyer and one seller. This is an extremely unusual situation; a very controlled (closed) economy might have this type of monopoly present.

Bilateral Trade: The free flow of goods and services between and among countries for the specific purpose of improving trade.

Bill of Exchange: A written document created by one party (maker or drawer) that orders a certain amount be paid to a third party (payee) by another (payer). This document is the same as a draft. A check (cheque) is also a form of a bill of exchange that is drawn on a bank account.

Bill of Lading: A document/receipt possessed by a supplier and provided by a carrier, that details the transport and transfer of goods to a buyer. No bill of lading means there is no delivery

Bill of Particulars: A document a defendant can request in a lawsuit which requires a written itemization by the plaintiff of the details of the claims to which the defendant is subject to in the lawsuit.

Bill of Sale: A document confirming that the sale of property, such as goods, possessions or a business, has been transferred to a buyer.

Binder: A written document that provides assuredness that there is adequate insurance coverage to both the insured and lenders, by providing the main and vital terms of an agreement to both these parties.

BIS: Acronym for the Bank of International Settlements, which was founded in 1930 as an international organization of central banks, whose role is to ensure monetary and financial stability worldwide. Many consider this to be the central banks' bank-owned by 29 central banks of various nations.

Blacklist: Refusing to hire labor union activists or others deemed undesirable because of their views or background. Blacklisting is not allowed under most labor laws and agreements.

Black Market: An illegal or underground market, where goods or services are sold, without financial records and without taxes being collected. Black markets exist for stolen goods, laundering currency, drug transactions or fake designer products.

Blank Endorsement: A situation where a check or negotiable instrument is endorsed, but the person to whom it is to be paid is not named on the document.

Block: For shares or bonds, a unit of 10,000 or more that is owned or traded.

Block Exemption: Basically an exception to E.C. competition laws which allows exceptions to Article 81 for such activities as vertical agreements, technology transfer agreements and research and development agreements.

Blue Sky Laws: In the United States, an effort to protect consumers and prevent individuals from investing in fraudulent companies that lack assets, these laws were created; they require that corporations get approval from the Securities and Exchange Commission or other state officials before selling or even advertising stock sales to the public. The corporations must present corporate financial and management information in order to gain approval.

Board for Actuarial Standards: Part of the Financial Reporting Council (FRC), it sets actuarial standards independently of the actuarial profession.

Board of Directors: Elected by, and accountable to, shareholders of a corporation, these individuals are responsible for setting the policies of the corporation and choosing its officers.

Boilerplate: A term referencing preprinted standard language within a written document that is common to that document and often is seen in similar documents word-for-word. In contract creation, whole paragraphs may be considered boilerplate and used repeatedly in other similar contracts.

Boiler Room: A term referencing a telephone telemarketing operation (often fraudulent) in which these individuals make it appear as though they are working from an established company in order to get the person they are calling to buy stock, services or goods.

***Bona Fide*:** A Latin term meaning good faith, with no intention to deceive. *See* PFP.

Bona Fide Purchaser: An individual that has purchased a promissory note, bond, other negotiable instrument or asset, and who is unaware of any facts which would call for uncertainty as to the right of the seller to have sold the instrument in any way but in good faith. Once, or if, the good faith of the purchaser is proved, then he or she can keep the instrument for its value and the real owner's only recourse is to go after the seller for recompense.

***Bona Fide* Resident:** An individual who meets the residency requirements of a foreign country; one who resides in another country legally.

***Bonas Vacantia*:** Property that is not owned, nor belongs to, any person, and which can be claimed by its finder, although some governments may lay ownership claims to all such property.

Bond: A written, interest-bearing document providing evidence of debt often issued by a company (as well as by a government), with the terms of payment laid out. This document provides predetermined payments to the bondholder, with a final payoff date stated.

Bonded Debt: Another term for funded debt, it is the fixed debt of a corporation or even a government. There may be other debt that is not bonded.

Book Account: A business ledger that keeps the account of a customer's debits and credits, and showing the amount due at any given time.

Bookbuilding: The marketing of a block of shares before determining the offer price. The bookbuilding period begins with the publication of a preliminary offering document (the red herring).

Book Debt: The total value of the outstanding debts to a business-referring to the sums owed a business for all goods and services sold. Loans may also be included in book debt.

Book Value: The value of stock of a corporation is determined by adding up the stated value of the corporate assets, as shown in the corporate records/books, and deducting all the corporation's debts/liabilities. Although this is a good way to determine the value, it may not be truly indicative of the actual value of the corporation or its shares as its assets may be overvalued or undervalued on the books.

Boom: Rapid expansion or growth in the economy; typically all segments experience the benefits of this economic activity. Generally, an increase for goods and services, increased stock prices and escalating real estate prices.

Boomerang Effect: Licensing of technology or some kind of innovation to an international company and is used by a completing company to the detriment of the developer/license owner.

Border Barriers: Literally physical attempts at the border to restrict the flow of goods from one country to another. The goal may be to assign duties or tariffs; more realistically, it is controlling the flow of illegal products, items which may present a health risk or which may have an adverse effect on agriculture or livestock.

Borrower: A person to whom money or other property is lent with expectation of repayment at a future time, usually with interest.

Bottomry: A mortgage contract whereby a ship and/or its freight are pledged as security for a loan for repairs, for new equipment or for the use of the ship itself. If the loan is not repaid, the lender can sell the security.

Boycott: An effort by an organized group to lessen the sale of goods and services of a company in order to pressure that company to change corporate policies or practices. Those supporting social changes, such as eliminating child labor in manufacturing or pollution of the environment, may use boycotts as an effective measure to influence policy.

BPN: Acronym for a building preservation notice whereby planning authorities in the United Kingdom can limit for six months any attempt to tear down an historically significant building, even though it is not on the national registry.

Breach of Contract: A situation where, without a legal excuse, there is a failure to adhere to, and perform, any terms of a written or oral contract.

The breaking of contractual responsibilities may include such actions as not completing a job, not delivering goods or the substitution of inferior goods, among other actions. If a suit for damages is based on a contract, proving a breach of the contract is a prerequisite.

Break Fee: If a deal falls through, a fee paid by the defaulting party for costs incurred to make the deal in the first place. This can be hard to enforce if this provision is not worded carefully in any signed document.

Bretton Woods Agreement: An agreement adopted by 44 nations at an international monetary conference which resulted in the creation of the International Monetary Fund (IMF) and the International Bank for Reconstruction and Development. The overall purpose was to encourage and build economic development throughout the world.

Bribery: Where money, or some other item, is given or taken in order to influence corporate or governmental officials in the performance of his or her duties. This act constitutes a crime.

Bridge Loan: Often called swing loans (especially in construction), they are loans made to meet a customer's needs until some more permanent financing can be arranged.

Bridge Financing: *See* ***bridge loan*** above.

Brief: A legal written document usually prepared by an attorney that details, through the use of statutes, case analysis, regulations, etc., the legal reasoning a suit is being brought before the courts.

British Investment Trust: Although the first real investment trust was begun in Switzerland in 1849, the investment trust concept gained wide acceptance in England and Scotland, thus the name. Like any good management company, the goals of these trusts were to get the highest return for its owners as safely as possible. Many early British investment trusts invested in American securities and various ventures throughout the British Empire.

British Private Equity and Venture Capital Association: *See* BVCA.

Broker: A liaison that acts to help facilitate contracts between a buyer and seller, for a commission. These brokers are often regulated and licensed and have a duty (as fiduciaries) to act in the best interests of the customer(s). Examples of brokers include, stock brokers, real estate brokers and insurance brokers.

BSP: *See* ***basic state pension***.

Bucket Shop: Typically a dishonest brokerage whose sole purpose is to sell shares or other commodities at an inflated price to unsuspecting clients.

Once shares are purchased, clients find that there is not a market for their investments and the price drops sharply.

Building and Loan: An older name for what is more commonly known today as a savings and loan association.

Building Preservation Notice: *See BNP*.

Bulk Sale: When a merchant-usually a retailer, wholesaler or other company with inventory-sells all or a sizable amount of their stock and equipment.

Bulk Sale Laws: Modeled after those in the Uniform Commercial Code (UCC), these state laws are in place to compel merchants that sell all or a sizable amount of their stock and equipment to publish a notice of the sale and to give creditors written notice that the sale is taking place. In addition, to allowing creditors to make claims against the money, these laws require an account be set up temporarily to store the funds from the sale so that claims, if any, can be made by the creditors.

Bulldogs: City name for international bonds sold in the United Kingdom.

Bullet: A loan taken out by a large, multinational corporation which will be paid off in one lump sum at the time of maturity, perhaps at the time of the sale of an asset or subsidiary, for example.

Bundesbank: The German central bank whose primary responsibility is to set interest rates and control the money supply in the economy.

Bureau of the Census: Established in 1902, the Bureau is required by the United States government to collect and disseminate statistical data on the demographics of the U. S. population.

Business: This term does not necessarily mean a company or corporation, rather it is any activity that is gone into for profit

Business Expansion Scheme: A program from the 1980s whereby investors where given a tax incentive to invest in qualifying trading companies.

Business Invitee: This is an individual entering a company's property for the express intent of doing business with the company, rather than someone simply crossing the premises. This label placed on the individual is important, because the business is liable to the business invitee for injuries upon them stemming from dangerous conditions on the company premises.

Business to Business: *See B2B*.

Business to Consumer: *See B2C*.

Buy-out: Purchasing of an annuity from an insurance company as a means to secure employee benefits when a company is winding up a pension scheme/plan.

Buy-sell Agreement: This is a contract that lays out the parameters for the purchase of the percentage of interest in a company-by the other owners-of a partner or shareholder that decides to leave the business.

BV: A private company in the Netherlands, as in a limited liability company.

BVCA: Acronym for British Private Equity and Venture Capital Association, the industry association representing some 370 members of the venture capital industry.

Bylaws: These are the written rules that lay out how a corporation, partnership or organization is to conduct itself. These rules, which must be formally adopted, often provide for the election of a board of directors and officers, and generally provide for meetings and setting up hiring procedures, notices and other corporate matters. It is important to distinguish bylaws from the articles of incorporation, as the articles only provide the basic outline of the corporation and its stock structure.

C

C Terms: A category of incoterms requiring sellers to arrange transportation or shipping, thereby taking on the risk in transit.

CAC: Acronym for Central Arbitration Committee, whose function is to rule on recognition or de-recognition of trade unions for the purpose of collective bargaining in the United Kingdom.

Cadbury Report: At a time of waning confidence in financial reporting by corporations and the ability of auditors to provide safeguards to investors, the report resulted in the creation of the Code of Best Practice on corporate governance.

Call: A term used to denote when a corporation requires that a stockholder pay on an installment or assessment on shares already owned by the stockholder.

Call Loan: Lending on a demand basis, meaning that either party to the loan can call the loan, i.e. terminate the loan at will.

Call of More: From the London Stock Exchange whereby the holder has the right to call for an additional amount of stock, at the same price, equal to the amount shown in the contract.

Call on Capital: Any demand for payment for issued shares which are only partly paid.

Calvo Doctrine: Legal disputes from international affairs affecting multinational corporations are handled by the judicial system in the foreign country where the dispute originated.

Cambistry: In foreign exchange, it is the science (or art) of determining the cheapest way of remitting sums to a foreign country.

Canadian Institute of Chartered Accountants (CICA): This is the national association of professional accountants which licenses accountants to practice in Canada. Like similar organizations worldwide, its goal is to maintain the highest standards for accountants and supports research and publishing in accounting.

Cancel: When dealing with business documents, this term means to void, rescind or destroy it. This, in effect, is a way to render the document void and unusable.

Cap: This is slang terminology meaning the maximum of something, such as if a contract for services allows for a cap on the amount paid for those services. Consumers understand a cap as a limit on adjustable-rate mortgages, for example.

Capital: This is a company's (corporation's or partnership's) or individual's basic assets. Although they can take other forms, these assets include equipment, actual funds and property, but it does not include inventory, payroll or stock in trade.

Capital Account: Not including inventory or the value of goodwill, this is a list, or record, of a business' basic assets.

Capital Assets: The owned property, equipment and funds of a business.

Capital Expenditure: Referring to the payment by a business for the essential assets of a business, such as fixtures, inventory or other property.

Capital Flight: The movement of assets or currencies from one country to another, typically in search of a better return on investment or the avoidance of taxes. Capital flight is often based on sudden, dramatic economic changes in the host country (devaluation of currency). Short-term losses are justified in anticipation of protection of capital and finding better long-term investments. Some capital flight may be illegal, e.g. money laundering or avoidance of legitimate taxes.

Capital Gains: In business terms, these represent profits made from capital transactions, or more simply, the difference between the original price paid for something and the price that it was sold for.

Capitalisation/Capitalization: The total number of shares and the total market value of all the shares are equal to the value of the firm, or its capitalization.

Capital Stock: The amount shareholders originally paid for the issued stock of a corporation. The value of this stock has no connection or relation to what the current value of corporate shares may be at a given time.

Capitalized Value: Where anticipated earnings are trimmed down to better embody a more realistic value, due to the fact that expected/projected earnings sometimes turn out to be less favorable than originally anticipated.

Captive Funds: Private equity funds, often associated with a bank or other financial institution.

Caribbean Basin Initiative (CBI): A government policy of the United States to encourage and stimulate private-sector business development in the Caribbean and in Central America.

Caribbean Common Market (CARICOM): A customs union of English-speaking countries in the Caribbean region.

CARICOM: *See* ***Caribbean Common Market***.

Carnet: A form which allows for the temporary importation of a product with no duty required-say samples for selling purposes.

Carrier: Where, by means of conveyance, property or people are transported in exchange for a charge by a person or company. The transportation system, and not the owner of the system, is the carrier. The two types of carriers are common carrier and personal carrier.

Carryback: Used in accounting, this is when a current year's tax credits, deductions or business losses are used to amend a previously filed year's tax return in an effort to reduce tax liability.

Carrying for Hire: Goods or people are transported for a fee. Whether the carrier has liability for safe delivery or is subject to regulation is to be determined by a company or the individual being transported.

Carrying on Business: Pursuing a particular occupation on a continuous and substantial basis.

Carryover: A term used in accounting, it means to use a current year's tax credits, deductions or business losses to apply to the next year's tax return in an effort to reduce tax liability.

Cartage: The costs of transporting goods, by truck for example.

Cartel: Where a group of companies join in order to monopolize a market. These companies form an agreement as to which will preside over each different area of operation within the newly formed monopoly.

Cash Alternative: In the United Kingdom, in the course of a takeover, the bidder can offer shareholders the choice of cash or the bidder's (buyer's) shares.

Cashier's Check: A document (check) issued by a bank, and drawn on the bank's own account, after funds were provided to the bank by a purchaser. This check states the name of the payee and, as well as the name of the buyer of the check (referred to as a remitter). Once this check is received it is considered the same as cash, as it is guaranteed by the issuing bank.

Cash in Advance: An agreement or business practice of paying for freight on merchandise before delivery.

Cashless Exercise: A means of exercising an option in an employee share option scheme whereby the employee exercises the option without paying the exercise price. Usually a bank or brokerage pays on his behalf.

Cash Tender Offer: Typically in the United States, a buyer of a public company offers a fixed price for the shares of the company being acquired. If sufficient shareholders accept the offer, the bidding company would then gain control of the firm.

Cash with Order (CWO): Prepayment of goods or merchandise before they are delivered to a customer or consumer.

Casualty: This refers to a loss, and this loss could not be foreseen and is often unavoidable, like a building being struck by lightning and destroyed by fire.

Casualty Loss: Used in taxation, it refers to a deduction that can be taken for loss due to damage caused only by an unexpected, unforeseen and/or an unusual event, such as a storm causing flood damage or other act of God.

Cause of Action: Having the right to sue another party, say for breach of contract or failure to perform as specified.

Caveat: This is a Latin term meaning let him beware and is used as a warning or to delineate that there is a possible problem. In Scottish law, a document lodged by a party to ensure that no interim order is pronounced without all parties being in attendance.

***Caveat Emptor*:** A Latin term meaning let the buyer beware. Often used in retail settings, this term is used to let the buyer known that they buy at there own risk, and should examine the product for defects before making a final purchase. Although this term is still applicable even if the product being sold is listed as is, under the doctrine of implied warranty, a seller is responsible for defects he knows about and which are not obvious through a routine inspection.

CBI: Acronym for Confederation of British Industry. *Also see* ***Caribbean Basin Initiative***.

CD: *See* ***certificate of deposit***.

Cease and Desist Order: In business, this is an order from the court or a government agency that requires the named business or organization to stop, or cease, from doing an activity that is shown by strong evidence to be harmful and/or contrary to the law. This order can be permanent, but it may also stand until a court can render a final judicial determination on the order.

Central Fund: An emergency fund by Lloyd's members as protection for policyholders in the even of a Name being unable to meet his obligations.

Certificate: Generally, an official document attesting to the truth or accuracy of something.

Certificate of Analysis: A formal document by an importer or government agency which states that the consignment of goods meets certain minimal standards of quality.

Certificate of Deposit (CD): A document that, using money deposited in a bank, is issued by a bank and pays a fixed interest rate for a specified period. Generally considered a very safe investment.

Certificate of Incorporation: Issued by some states, this document signifies a corporation's existence upon the filing of its articles of incorporation. Other states use the articles themselves as proof.

Certificate of Origin: A formal document attesting to the country of origin for manufactured goods.

Certified Check: Issued by a bank, this check confirms that the maker of the check has enough funds within the bank to cover the amount stated on the check. The funds on this check have already been set aside by the bank, so even if the maker writes more checks and draws more funds from an account, the funds stated on the certified check remain untouched.

CESR: Acronym for the Committee of European Securities Regulators.

CFI: *See* ***Court of First Instance***.

Chain of Title: Dealing with the ownership to real property, this traces the succession of title from the current owner to the original owner, and it can take the form of notations of deeds, foreclosures, judgments of quiet title, certificates of death of a joint tenant, and other recorded transfers.

Chancellor: An traditional English legal term, it refers to a judge who presides over a chancery court.

Change of Control: A clause which allows one party to terminate a contract (typically long-term ones) if the other party is taken over. Often used in joint ventures, where the identity and ownership of the first party is important.

CHAPS: Acronym for Clearing House Automated Payment System. A computerized payment system for clearing checks in the United Kingdom.

Chapter I Prohibition: From the Competition Act 1998, it prohibits any activity which would limit, restrict or prevent competition in the United Kingdom.

Chapter II Prohibition: Again from the Competition Act 1998, it prohibits any conduct which amounts to the abuse of a dominant position in a market if it affects trade within the United Kingdom.

Charitable Contribution: Used often within the confines of taxation as it can be used as a deduction from gross income, this is a contribution made to an organization created for the purpose of charitable or organizational advancement (such as a church, for artistic appreciation, education, etc.).

Charity: Often established to help those in need or to provide some benefit to the public, charities are usually corporations that follow strict state guidelines and require IRS approval.

Charter: Meaning the same as articles of incorporation, and is used by some governing bodies instead of the latter (i.e. corporate charter).

Chartered Accountants: Equivalent term in the United Kingdom for a certified public accountant, indicating that the individuals so designated are trained to practice public accounting.

Chartered Institute of Management Accounts (CIMA): A professional association in the United Kingdom, CIMA is a member organization of management accountants whose role is to prepare and analyze information helpful to management; in a business setting, this information is then used to plan and utilize all available assets to enhance the company or organization.

Chattel: Moveable items of personal property which are not real property (land), nor are they permanently attached to land or a building.

Chattel Mortgage: A mostly unused written document (*see* **UCC**), it gives an interest in movable property (not land) to guarantee debt payment or the execution of some other action. Consumer loans were secured by furniture and other personal property.

Cheque/Check: A written document that is a draft upon a specified account within a bank, where the maker or drawer (person signing the check and who has the account) has the bank pay the amount noted on the check to the payee.

Chinese Wall: Compliance with securities laws to ensure that information generated/created in one part of a company is not made know or otherwise used by another part of the company to enhance investment performance or as information shared with outside customers. Large law firms and investment banks are particularly concerned about this kind of protection.

CHIPS: Acronym for Clearing House Interbank Payments System, a computerized check clearing system; most Eurodollar transactions are cleared through CHIPS.

CICA: *See* ***Canadian Institute of Chartered Accountants***.

CIMA: *See* ***Chartered Institute of Management Accountants***

City Code on Takeovers and Mergers: Known as the takeover code or Blue Book, this is a set of statutory rules and general principles on takeovers in the United Kingdom.

Chose in Action: A claim or right to personal property not actually in one's possession, as opposed to property actually in one's possession (chose in possession).

Chose in Possession: *See* ***chose in action***.

Churning: Denotes when a stock broker or sales agent buys and sells large amounts of shares in an effort to generate increased sales commissions. This practice is not only considered unethical, but it is usually considered illegal as well.

CIF: *See* ***cost, insurance and freight***.

CITES: Acronym for the Convention on International Trade in Endangered Species of Wild Fauna and Flora, first adapted in 1963 by international governments as a means of protecting endangered species from worldwide exploitation. Although voluntary, it is one of the largest organizations of its kind and has been particularly effective in preventing economic exploitation of fauna and flora.

Civil Action: A legal, civil proceeding involving lawsuits and not criminal prosecution.

Civil Code: The statutes and laws that deal with lawsuits and negligence actions.

Civil Law: The body of law that encompasses all legal issues other than criminal law (i.e., contracts, family law, negligence, etc.).

Civil Liability: Dealing with lawsuits, this constitutes the potential responsibility handed down by the courts for payment of damages (or other court enforcement) to the individual or corporation victorious in the lawsuit.

Civil Wrong: As opposed to criminal wrong, this is a non-criminal wrong typically based on the denial of another party's rights.

Claim: Making a demand for something, whether it is money, property or some other right afforded by the law. Often this is made in writing and if the demand is not made it often leads to a lawsuit.

Claim in Bankruptcy: A written claim filed when a debtor files for bankruptcy. This claim is filed by creditors and the known creditors will receive a creditor's claim form and a written notice of the pending bankruptcy.

Class Action: A lawsuit in which members of a large similarly situated class are brought together in an action against a accused wrongdoer. One caveat is that this group must be sufficiently numerous that it is impractical for them all to be before the court individually; otherwise the group may not receive class certification.

Classic System: Corporate tax system in the Netherlands and the United States, for example, whereby tax paid at the corporate level is not credited to shareholders.

Clean Bill of Exchange: An undocumented bill of exchange, e.g. without a bill of lading, insurance certificates and so forth.

Clean Hands Doctrine: A doctrine of law requiring that an individual or corporation petitioning the court for judicial action must be free from unfair conduct or fraud with regard to the subject matter that the individual or corporation brings before the court

Clear Customs: The paperwork, documents and inspection of imported goods for entering into another country.

Clearing Agreement: An agreement between countries to facilitate international trade whereby the clearance and offset of claims are managed. Often clearing agreements are between a country with a strong currency and one with a weak currency.

Clearing House Automated Payment System: *See CHAPS.*

Clearing House Interbank Payments System: *See CHIPS.*

Clear Title: Where ownership of real property is free and clear from any current or past claims on the current owner's title.

Close Corporation: As permitted by law, a corporation is allowed to operate more informally than most other corporations (e.g., without requiring a meeting with the board of directors to make decisions for the corporation). This type of corporation has a limited number of shareholders and often they are comprised of family members who may even help run the business.

Closed Shop: A company, either by choice or union agreement, hires only union members, although it cannot require employees to become union members even in a closed shop.

COBRA: See *Consolidated Omnibus Budget Reconciliation Act.*

Code of Conduct on Transnational Corporations: A United Nations initiative specifying good corporate behavior for multinational companies.

Coinsurance: An insurance policy where the risk is taken on by both the owner and an insurance company, because under this policy an insurance company insures only a partial value of the property of the insured owner.

Collaborative Research Agreement: An agreement by which universities obtain sponsorship from industry to conduct research and earn revenue when the research is turned into commercial development.

Collateral: Property or currency which is pledged as a security to a creditor to secure a loan or a debt. If the debt goes unpaid the creditor then assumes the ownerships rights (or legal rights) to the property or currency pledged.

Collateral Loan: Typically, a short-term loan for which the borrower has deposited or assigned some kind of collateral security, e.g. bonds, stocks or title to real property.

Collateral Source Rule: This is a rule of law which states that money owed to a wronged individual in a suit for damages cannot be deducted by the person or persons who committed the wrong from the amount they owe simply because the victim of the tort received money from other sources. Often this other source is insurance benefits.

Collection Agency: A company hired by a creditor to seek out debtors in an effort to get them to pay the debts they owe. In the United States, these agencies are regulated by the federal Fair Debt Collection Practices Act.

Collective Bargaining: A broad term covering the negotiations of an employer or a group of employers with a recognized trade union. The subject of this negotiation may include some or all of the following: working conditions, hiring and firing, job security, pay, working hours, holidays, pensions, sick leave and more.

Collusion: At least two persons, or a company through its officers or employees, conspire through an agreement to commit a fraud to gain an unfair advantage over a third party, consumers or others. Price fixing is one example of an activity in which parties may be perpetuating this kind of fraud.

Color of Title: A party appears to have valid title to some property (either personal or real) but in fact there is no title or there is a critical defect in the title.

Comaker: A check or promissory note is signed by multiple people. In this situation each party that signs the document (each a comaker) is responsible for the entire amount due.

Combination: Business relationships that include such formal or informal groups as pools, cartels and interlocking directorates. Combinations are often consider agents of restraint of trade and generally, if recognized, are illegal or at the very least unethical.

***Comite Central d'Enterprise*:** A central works committee for multi-plant operations in France.

***Comite d'Enterprise*:** In France, a works committee in a simple enterprise or undertaking.

***Comite d'Etabslissement*:** A local level works committee in France.

***Comite de Group*:** A works committee where the employer is part of a group (as opposed to a simple employer).

Comity of Nations: A general legal doctrine whereby countries accept and enforce each others legal decision as a matter of courtesy or convenience. This acceptance of legal decisions is not necessarily based on law.

Commercial Frustration: Where a written or oral contract is entered into and then an unexpected and uncontainable event renders it impossible for one of the parties to the contract to fulfill his or her contractual duties. The other party to the contract may then rescind the contract without penalty.

Commercial Law: It is the area of law that covers the relations, rights and conduct of people and businesses engaged in sales, merchandising, trade and commerce. The Uniform Commercial Code, or UCC, has codified this body of laws, and for the most part, it has been adopted by most states in the United States.

Commercial Paper: A class of short-term negotiable instruments such as short-term notes, bills of exchange and/or acceptances resulting from business, industrial or commercial activity. They are assumed to be liquidated within 3 to 6 months.

Commingling: Where one party mixes his funds with the funds of another party; or a trustee inter-mingles funds from one trust with other trusts, for example.

Commission: In business, this is a fee paid to an employee or agent often as a result of that individual making a sale. This fee, which is different from a regular wage payment, is most often in the form of a percentage of the total sum of the sale.

Commissionaire: In European jurisdiction, a commissionaire is a go-between for a buyer and a seller, for which he receives a commission for his efforts. In the United States or the United Kingdom, a commissionaire is an agent.

Commission for Racial Equality (CRE): Although funded by the British government, it is not a government agency but rather a public body founded to handle matters of racial discrimination and to promote racial equality in general.

Commitment: A legal pledge or an agreement/contract involving financial responsibility, e.g. an obligation to pay.

Commitment Letter: A letter of offer by which a bank or other lending institution sets out that it is prepared to lend money. It is usually accompanied by a term sheet (setting out the terms of the loan). Once the commitment letter is signed by the borrower and returned to the bank, it is called the mandate.

Committee of European Securities Regulators: *See* **CESR**.

Commodity: Basic agricultural, mineral or other products, often unrefined, and typically sold by a broker or on an exchange devoted to commodities futures and options.

Common Carrier: Different from a personal carrier, this individual, company or public utility must be in the business of transporting people and/or freight, and this means of conveyance is fee based by that individual or company.

Common Counts: These claims, which are listed in a complaint, are brought as part of a lawsuit for debts and they are alleged together and have to be defended collectively. This list might contain claims for work performed, money loaned or advanced, debt for goods sold and delivered or for money due on an account stated or on an open book account.

Common Law: Based on custom and usage practices, this is the unwritten law of the United Kingdom. This form of law grows its basis from historical legal precedents developed over hundreds of years and is the basis for many of the laws today both in the United Kingdom, the United States and other countries.

Common Property: This term refers to real property owned by tenants in common, each of whom have an undivided interest in the whole property.

Common Stock: These are corporate shares that are distributed by the board of directors, and the dividends from these shares are calculated on a percentage of net profits. Those holding these shares often have voting rights. These are distinguished from preferred stock.

Community Property: Ownership of property, usually between a husband and wife, each as co-owners of all that was acquired after their marriage, but which may exclude certain properties before marriage or real property acquired by bequest. In the United States, there are nine community property states; this kind of ownership is regulated on the state level.

Commutation: Giving up a pension in exchange for a lump sum payment of equal value. In the United States, small pensioners are often bought out if the sum is less than $10,000 in order save administrative costs.

Company: Any business enterprise that is formed to make a profit. Although a corporation can be a company, not all companies are incorporated, because corporations often must use some term in its name to show that it is a corporation (e.g., incorporated, corp., inc., etc.). In the general sense, a company can also be a partnership, trust, association, joint venture, pool syndicate, sole proprietorship or unincorporated organization.

Compensation: This is payment for work or a service performed, and is usually in the form of wages, salary or commission, although it could be in the form of goods as well. This term may also refer to the amount an injured party receives following an injury or loss in order to make them whole; and it is often paid by the insurance company representing the party that injured the first party.

Compensatory Finance: An economic theory (Keynesian) that states that government fiscal policy should be organized and planned in order to promote economic stability by actively counteracting major business fluctuations.

Competition Committee: A legal body established in the United Kingdom under the UK Competition Act of 1998. Its purpose is to investigate matters of trade competition and will also hear appeals presented to it when decisions have been rendered.

Compliance: Adhering to the laws and regulations governing an enterprise, whether such compliance is mandatory or voluntary. Compliance could be within the law, government regulations, international trade agreements, in accounting or by agreement within an industry.

Compliance Officer: One individual (or more) is appointed within a firm to be responsible for all financial services compliance regulations. A compliance officer may also be appointed to handle separate matters, such as matters of competition or health and safety matters.

Compound Duty: A combination of ad valorem duty with some specialized duty as required by the custom's authorities for certain goods entering a country of destination.

Compound Interest: This represents the payment of interest to both the principal and the earlier accumulated interest, which adds to the sum paid for money use above simple interest. If compounded daily, monthly or quarterly this amount may increase exponentially.

Compromise: In business this often deals with contracts, and it is an accord between two or more opposing parties which allows each side to resolve a dispute and/or reach an amicable settlement where each side is flexible. This agreement prevents a problem from reaching trial, for example.

Concealment: Where information that should, under the auspices of good faith, have been disclosed but was withheld. This is a form of fraud, and under contractual terms, information concealed can be a cause to rescind the contract by the party who was misled, or possibly even a civil suit for fraud.

Concentration: The general notion under the E.C. Merger Regulations whereby two or more previously independent companies undertake a merger, with the possibility of limiting free trade and competition. Included in this legal concept are de-mergers, joint ventures or even the acquisition of a significant number of shares in a similar company.

Condemnation: A process by which a government (or government body) exercises its right of eminent domain in order to take control of private land for a public purpose (e.g., highways, schools, etc.). The government will make an offer to purchase the property, but if a purchase price cannot be agreed upon a condemnation suit will proceed and go forward anyway at a price decided on by the courts or an appraiser.

Condition: Stated within a contract, this is a contractual term that must be performed in order for the other party to the contract to have the duty to perform his or her responsibilities.

Condition Precedent: In contractual law, this is an occurrence that must take place before a party to the contract can carry out or perform his or her part of the deal. For example, paint supplies must be delivered to a site to be painted before the paint crew is required to begin work. The crew cannot meet its contracted obligations if the provider has not purchased paint to do the work.

Condition Subsequent: In contractual law, it is an occurrence or event that terminates a party's duty to perform or do his or her part for a contract. For example, if a supermarket closes and this supermarket has a contract with a supplier for beef, once closed the beef supplier will no longer be required to make contracted deliveries.

Conditional Sale: A situation where the sale of goods or property is only complete if specific conditions, agreed upon by the parties, are met. For example, a buyer will buy a piece of machinery if seller first fixes the machinery as agreed.

Conduit Principle: Usually related to tax law, it is the provision which allows certain tax characteristics through an entity to the owner of an entity-short-term capital gains pass through a partnership to the partners.

Confidentiality Agreement: Also know as a non-disclosure agreement (NDA), it assures all parties engaged in sensitive discussions (a merger, for example) that the information provided is strictly confidential and may not be used for any purpose other than intended. The information from these kinds of discussions is clearly not intended to be used for competitive purposes. Thus, information provided is on a need-to-know basis, should not be shared with others and must not be copied and returned in its entirety at the appropriate time.

Confiscate: To remove from someone their personal property or goods with or without legal right.

Confusingly Similar: This term is used within trademark law, and refers to when a trademark, logo or business name so closely mirrors an already existing trademark, logo or business name that it might cause the public to misidentify or confuse the two. If the two similar products or businesses are not directed at similar markets or geographical areas a claim for damages may not succeed.

Connected Company: If one or more persons have control of one or more companies, the companies themselves are said to be connected. Control of any company means that the individual or individuals directs the affairs of the company. A connected company may or may not a subsidiary of the first.

Conscious Parallelism: An unintentional, even coincidental, replication by a company of a competitor's action, like making special offers that are very similar or moving prices of certain products up or down as the competitor did. If the activity seems to have been done due to an active conspiracy between the two rivals, then this coincidental activity could be in violation of antitrust laws.

***Consensus ad Idem*:** This Latin term is used in contract law and means an agreement and/or a meeting of the minds of the parties.

Consent: To agree voluntarily to a proposal or to provide something willingly.

Consequential Damages: These are claimed or compensated damages in a lawsuit where the wrongful acts leading to the damages were the direct result of the easily predictable wrongdoing.

Consequential Loss: This kind of loss is not a direct result of a breach, but does result indirectly from the breach. Assume a new computer system is installed, but the system fails and the purchaser losses business as a result. The company will try to collect not only for the failed computer system but also for the losses directly related to the breach.

Consideration: A key element of contract formation, this represents the benefit for which an agreement is to be bargained for between the parties (i.e., given by one party in exchange for a promise by the other); the consideration must be of some value.

***Consiglio de Fabbrica*:** Works council in Italy.

Consign: A situation where goods are delivered to another and that person or business then sells or transports the goods of behalf of the delivering party. This is distinct from selling goods at a wholesale price to a retailer for resale.

Consignee: This is the term used to describe the individual or company holding the goods of another, which will be sold or transported.

Consistency: Often in accounting, but applicable to the law as well, a principle that states that conformity be used from one period (or situation) to another period, thus observers are able to make comparisons knowing that the same principle or rules were used over time.

Consolidated Omnibus Budget Reconciliation Act (COBRA): A federal law requiring employers to offer employees, as well as their spouses and dependents, continuing insurance coverage if their work hours are cut or they lose their jobs for reasons other than gross misconduct.

Consolidated Accounts: In the United Kingdom, the Companies Act lays down specific requirements for consolidated accounts-a single set of accounts showing the financial results from a group of companies, a holding company with subsidiaries, for example.

Consolidation: Within corporate law, this term is used to describe the combining together of two (possibly more than two) corporations in order to create one single company. The shareholders in the newly created company simply turn over their shares for equally-valued shares of the newly created business

Consortium: This is formed when a group of separate businesses/people come together for the sole purpose of working together to complete a project that, if done by just one member of the group, would be beyond their individual scope. For example, three separate companies come together to build a new shopping mall, with each company providing certain key areas of knowledge and expertise needed to finish the project.

Conspiracy: Two or more parties agree to perform illegal or subversive acts to the detriment of others.

Constructive Dismissal: Resignation of an employee under circumstances such that he is entitled to resign by reason of actions taken by the employer.

Constructive Eviction: This occurs when a landlord, through the use of non-legal methods, evicts a tenant from their home or apartment. These methods can include: changing locks, nailing windows shut or even changing an electronic key-code for entry into a building.

Constructive Notice: This term is a legal fiction, because it assumes an individual received notice, even though actual notice was never personally delivered to the individual. An example is when notice is placed in an approved newspaper, even if the person to whom the notice is meant to reach never actually sees the notice.

Consumer Protection Laws: Laws intended to protect consumers from substandard, hazardous and/or deceptively advertised products and/or services they purchase. These laws also encompass and protect against fraudulent sales practices, and they fall under both federal and state statutes and under agency protections.

Contenancy: Multiple persons have, at the same time, a viable interest in the same real property (tenancy in common, joint tenancy or tenancy by the entirety may be included within this term).

Contingencies: An uncertain existing condition which may cause a gain or loss to an enterprise, but will ultimately be resolved when one or more future events take place.

Continuous Employment: An employee must complete a specified, minimum period of continuous employment with an employer to be eligible for certain rights and benefits: unfair dismissal, redundancy payments, maternity pay and so forth.

Contract: A legally enforceable agreement between two individuals or entities which, when accepted, obligates each to do, or not do something. This agreement can be either written or oral (naturally, written holds up better in court if a dispute arises).

Contract for Services: A document used to appoint or otherwise hire a self-employed individual (such as a consultant) to carry out defined services. The relationship between the parties is not that of employer and employee.

Contractor: This term often means a person or entity that is in the construction business and enters into an agreement with another to erect a building or to aid in the installation of certain parts of the construction project. The general contractor is the individual in charge of the entire job, while subcontractors make up the general contractor's staff and are the ones who handle specific work. Subcontractors are only responsible to the general contractor, not the person who owns the property or is funding the construction.

Contract of Service: An employment contract by which a worker agrees to be paid a regular wage, work defined hours and therefore is considered an employee of the firm.

Contractual Compromise: Typically applied when a company is insolvent or filing for bankruptcy, this is an agreement compromising all of the company's debts and the cooperation of each class of debtors as to the final disposition of assets. Not any easy compromise to reach as each interested party wishes to regain the maximum from the available assets.

Contractual Measure of Damages: When there is a breach of contract, these are the damages awarded. Damages for breach of contract are subject to remoteness, causation and mitigation.

Contractual Retirement Age: Although a required retirement age is often not specified, in some industries or for certain positions (chief operating officer) a mandatory retirement age is part of a contract. Airline pilots, for example, have specific contractual retirement ages.

Contrary Opinion: A business or investment action that is different from the current, popular opinion-for example, buying real estate in a bad neighborhood or buying stocks when everyone is selling.

Contribution Holiday: If a pension scheme has a surplus over what is expected to be needed to meet its future obligations, the employer or employers may take a contribution holiday and not make further payments until and if further funds are needed to keep the pension scheme solvent.

Contributory: If a company is winding up, this person is liable to contribute to assets in order to pay off all creditors and other obligations. Contributories tend to be shareholders who have not paid for their shares in full or members of unlimited companies.

Control: This term is particularly important with regards to agency law, and it means the authority to direct, oversee and restrict the business dealings of a person and/or an entity.

Controlled Foreign Company: In the United Kingdom, this is a company that is resident outside of the country, controlled by persons who reside in the U.K. and the company is subject to lower taxes in the area in which the company resides.

Controlling Law: Under contract law, this means the laws of the state that the court will utilize to interpret and render its decision in disputes. For example, if an agreement states that the law of Florida controls and if a dispute arises, then even if the act occurred in another state Florida's law would control.

Convention on International Trade in Endangered Species of Wild Fauna and Flora: *See CITES.*

Conversion: Where the property of one person is converted by another person for that person's own use.

Convertibility: In the foreign exchange markets, the freedom of or the ability to exchange currencies.

Convey: Dealing with real property, this is when title to the property is transferred by written deed from a grantor to a grantee.

Cooperative: Where businesses, manufacturers and even farmers with similar interests form an association to work together to market and sell their products and/or services in a more efficient manner in order to share profits; these profits are shared and divided based upon the effort, capital or production contributed by each member

Co-partner: An individual who is a member of a partnership.

Copy: With regards to copyright law, this is a tangible thing that is reproduced and kept for a period of time. Copy also refers to the written or typed documents produced by an editor, writer or other business staff personnel. For example, a marketing employee might produce a document for business purposes, and this would be referred to as copy.

Copyright: The legal designation provided to the creator and owner of some type of creative work that provides that individual with the control over how the work is dispersed and used. These include: licensing the work, selling it, making copies of the work, performing or recording it, distributing it, etc. Copyrights are federally protected, and many, but not all, countries recognize international copyrights under the Universal Copyright Convention.

Copyright Notice: A notice provided by the recognized symbol for copyright (©), along with the author or creator's name and the date of publication, although the Berne Convention has decreed that a copyright notice is not required for all types of copyright protection.

Copyright Owner: This is often the creator or author of the copyrighted material and it is the person(s) or entity whose name(s) appears listed in the United States Copyright Office as the copyright owner (can also be someone with a part of the copyright transferred in writing).

Copyright Registration: This is not only an act to further help protect the rightful owner of a copyright from infringement, but it is also a required process by the United States Copyright Office if an owner wants to/needs to bring an action for redress before a court. Although a work, once created and fixed in a tangible medium of expression, has federal copyright protection, registration provides an extra shield when bringing an infringement action.

Corner: Complete or nearly complete control or monopoly of a commodity or security. In the past, several attempts were made to corner the silver market, for example. The ultimate goal is to dictate price and generally cornering is considered illegal as a monopoly or restraint of trade.

Corporate Agent: Individual or company which is empowered to act on behalf of another.

Corporate Opportunity: A business opportunity arises and a corporate official becomes aware of it because of his or her position within the corporation. Due to the fact that an official owes a fiduciary duty to the corporation, and because this knowledge belongs solely to the corporation, the official has a duty not to utilize this knowledge for his or her personal benefit. Improper use of this information can subject the official to damages owing to the corporation.

Corporation: A legal entity which permits a group of individuals to create an organization and become an artificial person so that it can pursue objectives, enter into contracts, sue and be sued, issue shares to raise funds, and do other activities in furtherance of the business, as it is empowered with legal rights usually only reserved for individuals. This business can be for profit, as well as organized as nonprofit.

Cosign: When another signature is placed upon a promissory note or other document that places shared liability on all individuals signing the document for the obligations required by the document.

Cost Bill: A document, or list, submitted by the winning party in a lawsuit to the court which details claimed court costs (limits have been placed on what can be included in these costs).

Cost, Insurance and Freight (CIF): This term signifies the entire cost to be paid on goods both purchased and shipped.

Cost of Completion: In contractual terms, this represents the entire amount of money needed to complete a job fully under a breached contract where the work was not finished, and the breach occurred, due to a failure to perform.

COT3: In the United Kingdom, an employment tribunal form used to record the terms of a settlement in an employment claim. COT3 is not a legal requirement.

Council of the European Union: This is the European Union's main decision-making body. It is the executive council with one representative from each of the member states. It has a wide range of policy sectors. The presidency rotates among members at 6 month intervals.

Counterfeits: Fraudulent, bogus or imitations of an original-frequently paper money, but coins, documents, wills, trusts, art or any item that has real value or potential value.

Counteroffer: A situation where a party is made an offer, either written or verbal, and in response proposes a new offer to the offering party (often done in contract negotiations). When a counteroffer is made it in turn rejects the original offer, making a new one.

Counterpart: A written document that is often one part of several written documents that help to make up a contract. Although a written offer and written acceptance to that offer are examples of counterparts to a contact, a contract may have several counterparts in its formation.

Countersignature: Typically on a check, but any business or legal document where another signature is given as verification of the first or as a requirement that two officers have signed on behalf of the organization (often because of the gravity of the document or the amount of money involved).

Course of Employment: Often used in workers' compensation claims, this is what an injured party might claim he/she was involved in (actively working their particular job) when an injury or accident occurred. In the converse, an employer may claim an injured party was not doing their job when an injury occurred, possibly nullifying liability.

Court of Customs and Patent Appeals: When appeals are made based on decisions by the U.S. Customs Court or the U.S. Patent and Trademark Office, this is the federal court that hears those appeals. The court sits in Washington, D.C. and is compromised of five judges.

Court of Equity: Under English common law these were separate courts that dealt with lawsuits and petitions requesting a certain remedy that was not simply damages (e.g., injunctions, specific performance). Over the years these courts have combined with courts of law, although bankruptcy courts still operate as courts of equity.

Court of First Instance (CFI): This is the appeals forum for decisions made by the European Commission. The court may review decisions, impose penalties but it also may reduce or cancel sanctions as well.

Covenant: These are often found in written contracts or written documents that deal with real property, and they constitute a promise in which the document signatories agree to do, or not do, a certain thing. In real property, covenants are often restrictive in that they may limit certain types of land use. Types of covenants include, but are not limited to: covenants of warranty, covenants not to compete, mutual covenants, covenants which run with the land and restrictive covenants.

Covenant Not to Compete: Often used in business dealings, this is an agreed upon term in a contract, for example when selling a business, in which the seller agrees not to form a new, competing business for a stated period of time and/or within a certain geographical location.

CPR 18 Request: A formal request for more information about a party's claim or documents-the detailed provision is set out in CRP 18.

CRE: *See* ***Commission for Racial Equality***.

Credit: The ability to buy with a promise to pay later; derived from the Latin, *credo*, meaning, I believe.

Creditor: This is the name of the entity (often a bank) or individual to which a debt is owed.

Credit Bureau: A company that mainly focuses on the gathering and dissemination of credit information of individuals and businesses. This type of for-profit company provides this information to those types of businesses that provide credit facilities, such as banks, mortgage companies, etc.

Creditor's Claim: This is a written claim that must be proper in its form and properly filed by an individual or business that is either: owed money by a debtor who has filed a petition in bankruptcy court or had a petition filed to declare the debtor bankrupt; or is owed money by a person who has passed away. A creditor's claim in the estate of a person who is deceased must be printed in a legal advertisement giving notice of death.

Credit Insurance: Often required by lenders, this is insurance that protects against the risk of nonpayment of a commercial debt. Basically, this policy will pay the remaining balance if a business becomes insolvent or if the borrower becomes incapacitated and cannot make the loan payments.

Credit Scoring System: An analytical, statistical and completely impersonal way to judge an individual's credit worthiness. Such systems are based on amount of debt owed, length of time on the job, years at the same residence, payment history and so forth. The system may never incorporate any issues of age, sex, race, religion, and so forth.

CREST: The electronic securities system of the U.K. and Irish securities markets. Shares can be held and transferred as well electronically.

Cromme Commission: The German government appointed a commission to write a new corporate governance code. The final version from the Cromme Commission was completed in 2002.

Cross-default Clause: In the context of a loan agreement, default by the borrower on any debt owed to the lender will be considered a default on the current loan between the parties.

Cross-licensing: This is a business arrangement whereby different companies share patent rights with each other through licensing agreements. This provides each company with a right to use the other's patented material.

Crowding Out: The limitations or inability of the private sector to borrow on the open market because government, through debt financing, has consumed the greater share of available credit for its needs.

Crown: Referring to the British Monarch because it is the head of state; prosecutions and civil actions brought by the government are taken in the name of the Crown. In Canada, for example, prosecutors are called Crown prosecutors and criminal cases are taken as The Crown vs.

Cumis Counsel: This is an attorney that is retained by an insured defendant in a lawsuit where there is an insurance policy, but the insured needs to retain his/her own counsel because the insurance company and the insured individual have a conflict of interest.

Custodianship: Accounting for and safekeeping of something of value for another; an adult may have custodianship of a minor child's assets until she becomes of age to manage her own assets and real property.

Custom and Practice: In the context of employment law, these are implied customs or practices, recognized by both parties, even though they are not formally part of the employment contract between employer and employees.

Customs: The laws and regulations that deal with imports and exports.

Customs Court: This federal court hears appeals stemming from decisions made by customs officials regarding categorization and classification of merchandise, duty rates and also interpretation of customs laws; and the decisions made by this court can also be appealed to the Court of Customs and Patent Appeals.

Cut a Check: Writing out and then signing a check.

CWO: *See* ***cash with order***.

D

Damages: An amount of money in which a plaintiff in a lawsuit may recover. Types of damages include: special damages (medical bills), general damages (pain and suffering) and punitive damages (awarded to punish an offender for acting in a malicious, violent, oppressive, fraudulent, wanton or grossly reckless way).

Danger Pay: Some types of employment carry extraordinary amounts of risk and employers are compelled to pay additional wages to fill these positions. Postings in foreign countries in times of war, for example, may require danger pay to attract workers in order to fill these open positions.

Data Room: As part of an auction, the seller puts together a physical data room where information about the targeted company is gathered for all interested parties to review. A virtual data room can also be collected and published electronically.

Dawn Raid: In the United Kingdom, a surprise inspection by government bodies at a company's premises whereby the officials at the competition authority have concerns about a company's business practice.

Days of Grace: Deferring payment of a note or an obligation after the original due date; in the United Kingdom, 3 days of grace have traditionally been allowed and if payment is then received, the account is said to be paid on time.

DBERR: *See* ***Department for Business, Enterprise and Regulatory Reform.***

DDA: Acronym for Disability Discrimination Act of 1966 which prohibits discrimination disability relating to employment; it further guarantees access to goods, facilities, services and premises without prejudice as to a handicap.

DDA Questionnaire: This device is used in the United Kingdom by those who feel that they have suffered discrimination (based on disability) to gather information from the alleged discriminator. This, then, can form the basis for making a decision on whether to bring an action or not against an employer, for example.

Deadlock: When individuals to an agreement have irreconcilable conflict; for example, a joint venture with each party owning 50 percent of the shares and they are unable to reach a decision, one way or the other. A well-written joint venture agreement has some kind of common deadlock provision written into the text to solve such problems.

Dealer: An individual who's business is to buy goods or property with the express purpose of selling the goods or property. A dealer is different from just a casual buyer and seller, as this professional often needs to secure a business license to operate, register with sales tax authorities and cannot defer capital gains taxes when property is sold.

Debenture: Any form of unsecured, long-term debt, whether corporate or civil. In the United Kingdom, a debenture is often secured with a mortgage deed of some kind.

Debt: An amount of money, value of property or services owed by one to another. Credit provided by a seller to a buyer most often results in debt.

Debt Agreement: A loan is made between a lender and a borrower under which money is lent under specific conditions or covenants. The agreement often covers what happens in the event of default or failure to maintain one or other covenants.

Debt for Equity Swap: Often used in company reorganizations, creditors will convert debt into ownership (equity) of the company. The overall goal is to take an almost hopeless situation and try to salvage something from a bad debt circumstance. Further, without the obligation to pay principal and interest on the debt, the company has a chance to survive the reorganization.

Debtor: This is the person, persons or business that is obligated to pay back money to another to extinguish the debt. Also, in bankruptcy this is the person, persons or business whose affairs are the subject of the proceeding.

Debtor in Possession: This is a term used in bankruptcy proceedings in which a debtor has filed for the right to submit a reorganization and refinancing plan under Chapter 11 bankruptcy, but is still allowed to manage the business without an appointed trustee.

Debtor in Possession Finance: Most frequently used in the United States, it is new financing given to a company that is under the protection of the courts in some kind of bankruptcy proceedings. Repayment of the new money always takes precedence over other debt, thus it is senior debt.

Debt Relief: Any type of forgiveness of debt by a lender; most frequently seen in international finance where institutions forgive a loan to a third-world country in an effort to stimulate economic activity.

Deceit: Often dishonest, fraudulent statements made to another knowing that the statement is false, and knowing that this false statement will be believed and relied upon by another. This is a civil wrong and can lead to a lawsuit if the deceived individual(s) relied on these fraudulent statements to the point of injury.

Deceptive Practices: Any activity designed to fool the consumer, for example using false advertisements, making unfounded claims about a product's features, deceptive packaging or misstating information. All of these and similar activities are illegal.

Declaration: In terms of dispute resolution, it is a court decision setting out the rights or legal positions of the parties. It is usually appropriate if the matter affects a large number of parties.

Deduction: For tax purposes, this is an expenditure that an income tax payer may subtract from his or her total income. This helps determine the taxable income.

Deed of Arrangement: Individuals debtors will make formal arrangements with their lenders in place of bankruptcy. It is also called individual voluntary arrangements.

De Facto Corporation: This is a company that operates as a corporation even though it has yet to finish the legal process required to become a corporation (e.g., filed its articles of incorporation); or it is a company that continues, despite being suspended or dissolved, to operate as a corporation. In order to avoid harming individuals who acted and believed that the company was a corporation, the courts will often treat it as a legal corporation.

Defalcation: This Latin term, meaning deduction, refers to the misappropriation or withholding of funds by an individual or entity (often a public official), or failing to make a proper accounting of the funds.

Defamation: Often of character, one individual publishes a statement which lowers the public's estimation of another person. The test of defamation is whether it would cause one to think less of an individual or company.

Default: Inability, unwillingness or failure to pay back an obligation, note, debt or IOU, including all principal and any interest due. By contract, the debtor typically has recourse, such as seizure of property held as security or taking the debtor to civil court seeking relief.

Default Risk: The likelihood or degree of probability that a debtor will fail to make interest and principal payments on a loan on a timely basis or at all.

Defeasance: This is an term relating to a document that works to terminate the effects of an existing document or writing (e.g., a contract or deed) if a certain event occurs.

Defect: A situation where some type of good or writing has an imperfection that often renders the good or writing ineffectual. For example, if a boat has a large whole in it, this is a defect; or if a contract for the sale of a car is signed by someone that does not own the car, this too can be a defect. Minor defects, which do no render the goods or writings without use but only limit their value, may not terminate the sale or writing depending on the circumstances.

Defendant: In civil suits, these are the individuals being sued for money or other damages. When dealing with criminal cases, these are the individuals being charged with a crime.

Deficit: Basically more liabilities than assets; in business, a debit balance in the retained earnings column.

Defined Benefit Plan: A pension plan created by an employer, who typically pays most of the cost for setting up and maintaining the plan, in which contributions are made on an actuarial basis in order to provide a specific, defined benefit, e.g. 70 percent of base income upon retirement. These kinds of plans are increasingly rare, as the cost is unknown and they are often unfunded, leaving an obligation to various government agencies to fill the gap.

Defined Benefit Scheme: *See* ***defined benefit plan***.

Defined Contribution Plan: Unlike a defined benefit plan, a specific contribution to an investment plan by both employees and employers is made; only the contribution is defined (agreed to) with the ultimate outcome unknown because of years of service, the quality of the investments made and other market risks.

Defraud: To makes false statements and use trickery to obtain money or rights from another individual or entity.

De Jure Corporation: Different from a de facto corporation, these are corporations in good legal standing.

Del Credere Agent: A principal required his agent to guarantee the debts of customers whom he finds for the principal and with whom he concludes agreements on behalf of the principal.

***Delegues du Personnel*:** In France, delegates elected by staff members when the company employs 11 or more employees.

Delegues Syndicaux: Representatives of a trade union in France.

Delinquent: When a payment due is not paid in full or on time.

Deliver: To in fact physically hand a document, money or other item to another.

Delivered Prices: An unusual practice of delivering goods at a single, stated price (including delivery charges) regardless of the location of the customer. The effect is to discriminate against certain customers.

Demand Note: A promissory note that provides its holder with the ability to seek payment on it at anytime; it is in contrast to a note that is due payment by a certain date, by installments or when a certain event occurs.

Demerger: A spin-off, or when a company splits into two or more separate companies. New shares are issued for existing shareholders of the original company. Often a demerger is used to gain greater value for shareholders.

***De Novo*:** Latin term meaning anew, or to start over. In legal settings, this is often used when a decision is appealed from one court to another (e.g., small claims court decision is appealed to a trial court), and the new court tries the case again, *de novo*, or anew.

Department for Business, Enterprise and Regulatory Reform (DBERR): Department of government in the United Kingdom and generally is responsible for promoting business in the U.K. It is concerned with business relations, regional development, fair trade and energy policy, for example.

Depletion: Descriptive of the mining, oil, gas and forestry industries, it is the exhaustion of the assets. A depletion allowance is generally created so that when the assets are depleted, money is held in reserve to pay for cleanup, reforestation or payment to the original owners.

Deposition: Process, before trial, by which witness testimony is taken under oath, away from the court, and recorded by a court reporter. It may be used for trial preparation and in the trial itself.

Depreciation: A process by which an asset gradually loses value, actually or theoretically, over time or by natural wear and tear. Often this process is seen in the value of business equipment or in a building, and it may be used for business income tax reduction

Depreciation Reserve: A business fund set up with the express purpose of accumulating the estimated replacement cost of a piece of equipment over time so that it can be replaced when needed.

Derivative Action: An action (lawsuit) brought forth by a shareholder of a corporation against the directors, management and/or other shareholders for a failure by management to exercise their authority in the best interests of the corporation and its shareholders. This lawsuit is brought on behalf of the corporation by the shareholder. Often, these suits arise due to claims of fraud, mismanagement, self-dealing and/or dishonesty.

Derivative Work: When dealing with copyright law, an original work of authorship is created when a new piece of work, based on an original piece of work, has enough unique, creative ideas put forth in it that it is distinguished from the original. An example is when a screen play is adapted from a book and made into a movie.

Designated Investment: A security or contractually-based investment, such as a life insurance policy or pension scheme.

Designated Professional Body: In the United Kingdom, a professional society under the Financial Services and Markets Act 2000, such as Law Society, the Association of Chartered Certified Accountants, the Institute of Actuaries, The Council of Licensed Conveyancer, and so forth.

Determination: For customs purposes, the origin of merchandise and any major components of the merchandise for assessment of duties on imports.

Devisen: Foreign bills, checks or balances, derived from the French, *devise*.

Digital Watermark: Embedding information (a copyright) into a digital work much the same way as a watermark embeds an image on paper. The intent is to protect the work from reproduction or use by another without the owner's permission or without the payment of a fee or license.

Dilution: When a trademark and/or a service mark is used in a situation that may be damaging to the reputation associated with that mark. When infringement is used, dilution is not, and visa versa.

Diminution of Value: This refers to the decrease in the value of property upon a breach of contract due to the failure to build to exact specifications as to what was laid out in the contract.

Director: These elected positions of a governing board of a corporation are in charge of making certain policy decisions (e.g. leasing a new office, borrowing money) for the company, and many of these decisions are legally binding on the corporation, although the day-to-day operational decisions are usually left to managers/officers. Elections for this position are often held at annual meetings of the shareholders and most regulatory bodies require at least three directors on corporate boards.

Directeur Departemental de Travail: In France, the Labor Inspection Department.

Disability: A condition, which can be temporary or permanent, that might preclude an individual from completing all the usual functions and tasks associated with his employment. Laws require that individuals with disabilities be accommodated both in the work place and outside of it.

Disability Discrimination Act: *See DDA.*

Disaffirm: To repudiate an arrangement, such as declaring that one party is not bound by an illegal or fraudulent contract.

Disaster Recovery Plan: For a business, it is a written statement on what is to be done before (to prevent a problem), during and after a disaster such as a fire, flood or loss of a computer system. The goal is to continue operations at the same or next best level as soon as possible and to repair all systems. The single most important part of a disaster recovery plan are those steps taken to prevent a loss of business function, such as redundant computer systems, backup files and so forth.

Discharge: To release a party from an obligation, contract or loan; also the payment of a loan. In employment law, to be fired from gainful employment.

Discharge in Bankruptcy: Where the bankruptcy court issues an order at the conclusion of the court processing of a bankrupt person's assets and debts, thee debts that cannot be paid are forgiven. There are exceptions to this order, as debts for illegal actions, alimony and child support, as well as taxes, cannot be discharged.

Disclaimer: A refusal to accept responsibility for loss or damages; a renunciation or repudiation. Also, to renounce a claim or right.

Disclosure: Generally in financial or contractual matters, that all pertinent facts are made available to the parties involved. No pertinent matter has been keep from a lender or borrower, for example.

Discount: When dealing with promissory notes, this is the payment of less than that which is required due; for goods or services, less than the full quoted price. This reduction in price is most often agreed to by the parties.

Discount Rate: Typically the rate of interest a bank charges it customers; sometimes called bank rate. The best customers, under the best economic conditions get the best discounted rates.

Discrepancy: A disagreement about the material facts or claims made by two parties. Also, the difference of what is expected and what actually takes place or what is actually paid versus what was expected to be paid.

Discrimination: In most societies, this is unfair treatment or denial of rights or privileges based on race, age, sex, nationality or religion. It is the granting of favor or privileges on a preferred class to the determinant of others.

Dishonor: The refusal of a party provided a check or promissory note to pay the face amount specified or due under the note. Otherwise known as dishonor for nonpayment.

Dissolution of Corporation: When a corporation dissolves, or terminates, by terms that are voluntary, involuntary, by payment of debts, by resolution, by distribution of assets, by filing the suitable documents with the state, by state action, and for committing some prohibited corporate offense.

Distinctive Mark: When dealing with trademarks or service marks, these are the marks that are so memorable because of their remarkable or unusual use within a certain context. These types of marks get the utmost protection under federal and state laws.

Distribute: For business purposes, this term refers to the dividing up of profits and/or assets of a business.

Diversion: Changing the billing rate for transporting goods after being shipped but before the goods are delivered to the buyer.

Diversity of Citizenship: This situation arises when parties reside in different states or when a party resides in a foreign country-this includes corporations incorporated or doing business in other states-and a lawsuit is brought. If the lawsuit exceeds $10,000, then it will fall under federal court jurisdiction in the United States, for example.

Divesture: Often used in antitrust actions to prevent monopolies or other attempts at restraint of trade, this is the process by which a possession or right is given up, either forcefully through a court order, or voluntarily.

Dividends: Payments which are distributed to shareholders for each share they own, and are based on a portion of a corporation's profits. Although they can be paid in money, the can also be paid to shareholders in shares of stock-called a stock dividend.

Division: A business unit that is separate from the rest of the company; it may operate as though it were a stand-alone company even though it is part of a larger organization.

Division of Labor: An economic theory, traced to Adam Smith in his *Wealth of Nations*, that specialization of labor produces efficiencies in manufacturing. Often considered the theoretical basis for the modern assembly line where one person performs one task only.

Doctrine of Equivalents: An existing patent right is violated by a new invention that does very similar work in a similar way and achieves the same result that the original patent produced.

Doctrine of Sovereign Immunity: Because of coercion of a foreign government, an executive of an international corporation will claim immunity as a defense in an act which violates the law of the home country.

Documentation: Supporting evidence to a statement or claim; cancelled checks are documentation of payment of a loan.

Domestic Content: A government requirement that a portion of imported goods include a percentage of parts or labor produced by the receiving country. The general goal is to ensure that domestic jobs and companies are protected.

Domicile: For business purposes, a business is domiciled in the state/country where its headquarters resides.

Dormant Company: A firm which has not carried out any significant business (accounting transactions) since its formation or since the end of the previous financial year.

Double Dipping: In terms of compensation, an executive participates in more than one kind of share incentive agreement, each rewarding the same performance measures.

Double Taxation Treaty: International agreements whereby corporations are granted tax relief, thus not liable for taxes for the same earnings in two countries. Taxes on royalties in one country are deducted, but the earner may seek relief from the second (home) country by demonstrating that the tax was already paid.

Downsizing: An effort to streamline a company and improve productivity or reduce costs by cutting the number of employees or closing work locations (plants and offices).

Draft: In business financial terms, a written document, or order, that provides for one party to pay another. Examples are bills of exchange and checks. The writer of the draft is called the drawer, while the individual or entity with the money (e.g., a bank) is referred to as the drawee. The individual or entity who will receive the money is called the payee.

Drag Along Rights: In the articles of association (incorporation) if a majority of the shareholders (typically 75 percent) agree to sell, the remaining shareholders are forced to accept the offer as well. Thus the buyer is assured of 100 percent ownership of the company.

Dram Shop Rule: Adopted by statute or case law in 38 states in the United States (and similarly in most western countries), this provision holds businesses or hosts who serve or sell alcoholic beverages to people who are clearly intoxicated strictly liable to anyone who might be injured by the drunken individual.

Draw: To set-up and prepare (sometimes also sign) any type of written document. For example, to prepare a bill of exchange or check.

Drawee: The individual who is to be paid on the draft (e.g., check or bill of exchange) signed by the drawer. This title can also designate the person that will receive the money, but often they are referred to as the payee.

Drawer: The person that prepares and signs the draft (e.g., bill of exchange).

Drawstop: In any loan agreement, should a breach occur, the lender has the right to refuse to make further loans or advances.

Drop Dead Date: This is a condition within a contract or court order that specifies what the last date is for an event to occur or take place (e.g., making a payment) before automatic consequences go into effect, such as contract cancellation or foreclosure.

Drop Hands: A settlement agreement under which parties will bear their own costs.

D Terms: Obliges seller to deliver to a stated place, i.e. the seller to procure and pay for the goods to a nominated point.

DTI Investigation: In the United Kingdom, a Department of Trade investigation allowed under the Companies Act by which a company or its directors are to be investigated for misconduct, such as intent to defraud creditors, actual fraud, misfeasance or other misconduct.

Due: Used often when referring to debt, this is the specific date when something owed must be brought forth.

Due Diligence: The process of uncovering and verifying all pertinent facts about a business and confirming what has been provided by management. For example, that the assets are as described and the debts of the company are fully stated.

Due Process: A means designed that laws and regulations are not administered or interpreted arbitrarily. It is the expectation that the administration of law will be usual and ordinary.

Dummy: Often used in context of a corporation that has no real function or control over a business' affairs. A person who acts for another but has no real power.

Dumping: Setting prices below the cost of production and selling the same goods on the open market or to foreign countries for less than their worth. This is generally considered an unfair trading practice and subject to anti-dumping penalties and tariffs in order to make up the difference.

Dutch Auction: Open bidding for goods or real property whereby the auctioneer starts at the highest expected price and goes down from there until a buyer is found.

Duty: In contracts, this is a legal obligation contracted for, and if not done and a breach occurs, then liability could attach. This term also refers to a tax on imports.

Duty of Good Faith: A business practice in continental Europe whereby good faith exists on the parties entering into a business arrangement. Each party to a potential deal informs the other about important issues affecting the business transaction and a general agreement to act ethically.

Duty Reimbursement: Duties for imported goods are refunded because the goods are then exported; a common situation may be when the goods imported are components of larger, manufactured products.

E

Early Neutral Evaluation: This is just one kind of alternative dispute resolution. While it is not binding, the hearing judge offers his opinion as to how the matter will play out in court. The parties to the action then get an indication as to the probable outcome of their complaint.

Earn Out: Part of the purchase price of a business is based on the future performance of the business being purchased. Often this is used as an incentive to keep the owner/manager involved in the business following the sale. It is to her best advantage for the business to do well as her buyout price will be higher if over the next year or two if sales increase. The sale price of the business is tagged to this future increase.

Earnest Payment: A partial payment submitted to show commitment to a contract and often to bind the parties to the contract. The remainder that is left over after the partial payment (or deposit) will be due under the contract agreement at a later, specified time. If the party providing the partial payment breaches the contract by not paying the final amount then the other party may keep the partial payment as liquidated damages.

Ease: To facilitate something; to make it easier for one party to do business with another. To mediate on behalf of an individual or a corporation.

Easement: The right to use land that belongs to another for a specific purpose, for example an easement to run electrical cables underground to service customers; or the right to enter one property to get to another. No transfer of ownership takes place.

EBRD: Acronym for the European Bank for Reconstruction and Development, which was founded in 1991. Its purpose is to build market economies and to promote democracy in Eastern Europe and Central Asia. The bank is owned by over 60 countries and works primarily with private companies and investors on a variety of commercial projects.

ECMR: Acronym for European Community Merger Regulation which requires prior notification to the European Commission about mergers, acquisitions and certain joint ventures that involve the change of control of one of the parties.

Economic Integration: A conscious governmental effort to expand trade and financial services among nations, such as the European Union. Greater regional integration will lead to more efficient systems and businesses, thus creating economic prosperity for the region.

Economic Nationalism: Essentially the opposite of economic integration (*see above*). This theory suggests that markets should be closed to foreign imports and that foreign ownership of businesses should be sharply curtailed as a means of protecting national, political and financial institutions.

Economic Sanctions: Often used as a political weapon to force change within a country, this is a system whereby business and financial restrictions are imposed by one nation (or a group of nations) on another nation or group of nations.

Economic, Technical or Organizational (ETO): If an employee in the United Kingdom is dismissed because of a transfer of the business, it will not be allowed as a justified termination unless the employer can show an economic, technical or organizational reason for the business transfer, and thus the employee termination.

Economic Zones: Special areas of a country set aside for economic development, offering companies within the zone and companies doing business with companies in the zone favorable treatment-reduction of duties, for example. China has one of the largest economic zones in the world.

Economic Theory of Pricing: Demand for goods and services is a direct function of price, taste, income and competition. Generally, the higher the demand, the higher the price that can be asked. Conversely, price will decrease to a point where there is demand at that price.

EC Regulation: This is a legal instrument of the European Community which has legal standing in all member states and without further action by the member states shall be in force equally and for all members.

EDF: Acronym for the European Development Fund, which was founded in 1957 as part of the Treaty of Rome. The purpose of the fund is to provide technical and financial assistance to African, Caribbean and Pacific Rim countries.

EDGAR: Acronym for Electronic Data Gathering, Analysis and Retrieval of the U. S. Securities and Exchange Commission. The role of EDGAR is to ensure the efficiency and fairness of the financial market; that all information about companies be made available to every interested party.

EDIFACT: Acronym for electronic data interchange for administration, commerce and industry. This is an United Nations directive toward developing an international standard for electronic data interchange.

EDX London: An equity derivative exchange established in 2004 by the London Stock Exchange and the OM London Exchange Limited.

EEC: *See* ***European Economic Community***.

Ejusdem Generis: Latin term meaning of the same kind. It is used when interpreting loosely written statutes.

Elective Resolution: In the case of a private company (privately-held) in the United Kingdom, members/owners can pass a resolution dispensing with certain administrative requirements of the Companies Act of 1985. An example is to drop the requirement to hold an annual meeting.

Electronic Data Gather, Analysis and Retrieval: *See* *EDGAR*.

Electronic Data Interchange for Administration, Commerce and Industry: *See* *EDIFACT*.

Electronic Funds Transfer: Funds are moved from one account to another via terminal, telephone, computer or magnetic tape-in other words, any way possible with the exception of exchanging paper money.

Electronic Signature: This refers to how a party can agree to the terms of a wholly electronic contract. There are various ways for a party to sign an electronic document for purposes of binding the parties to the contract (e.g., typing his/her name into a predetermined box, clicking a button [I Accept] or use a key encryption program). The Electronic Signatures in Global and International Commerce Act determined that electronic signatures are as binding as those in ink.

Embargo: A government or administrative order preventing ships or cargo from coming into or leaving a country. Also a request that a news organization hold back from reporting information until a specified date.

Embezzlement: A crime committed by an employee against his/her employer, where money or property is stolen by the employee, or money or assets held in a trust are misappropriated.

EMI Options: *See* ***enterprise management incentive options***.

Eminent Domain: A power afforded the government to take private land for public purpose, without the land owner's permission. Just compensation must be paid to the land owner once the land is confiscated for public use.

Emolument: A term meaning the salary, wages and benefits paid for employment or an office held.

Employee: An individual hired by an employer to perform work duties for a fee, salary or wage. When dealing with agency law the employee is often referred to as the agent and the employer is the principal, and whether an agent is acting within the scope of duties for the principal is an important determination, because if the agent is, then liability can attach for damages they may have caused.

Employee Retirement Income Security Act (ERISA): This federal law in the United States was enacted to regulate private pension plans, and it provides workers with some protections if the plan itself cannot pay out the benefits entitled to the employee. The law also requires employers to provide full information to their employees about their pension rights, and employers' must ensure that the administration of the funds within the pension is transparent and prudent.

Employer: A person or business that hires employees and provides payment and benefits to them. Under agency law they are often referred to as principals.

Employment Tribunal: In the United Kingdom. formerly called industrial tribunals, by law the tribunal is empowered to hear and rule on employment disputes.

EMS: Acronym for the European Monetary System, an agreement established in 1979 whereby most countries of the European Economic Community (EEC) agreed to link their currencies to prevent large fluctuations in valuation.

Enabling Act: Legislation in the United Kingdom that permits local communities to organize into larger districts in order to build public works for the betterment of all the communities, e.g. schools, sewers and water works.

Encryption: Converting data, information, text, images or sounds into another form so as not to be read or copied by an unauthorized third party. Almost all e-commerce on a Website uses encryption as a means to protect customer credit cards, for example.

Encumbrance: A claim or lien on personal or real property; a mortgage is an encumbrance on an owner's piece of property and limits his use or disposal of that property.

Endorsement: In the financial industry, the act of an owner or payee placing his or her signature on the back of a check, bill of exchange or other negotiable instrument. This signature makes the instrument payable to another party or cashable by the holder of the document. There are both qualified endorsements (pay to the order of Sue Smiles) and blank endorsements (no instructions and payable to the holder).

End-use Tariff: A fee placed on imported goods based on how they will be used ultimately; goods used by a charity for fund raising may have an end-use tariff that is different than goods imported for sale and profit.

Enforced Self-regulation: Any kind of code of conduct or code of best practices adopted by a group (accountants, for example) and have government approval. In effect, they become enforceable by law.

Enjoin: A situation where a court orders that someone or some entity stop a course of action or that they are prohibited from committing a certain act. This type of order by the court can also require someone or some entity to do a certain act.

Enroute Expenses: Typically reimbursement of expenses for managers and officers of a company with international offices or facilities, including travel, hotel, food and entertainment costs incurred in the normal course of business. These expenses would be outlined in an employment agreement signed by both the company and the employee.

Enterprise Management Incentive Options: Often called EMI options for short, the options have a tax advantage in the United Kingdom to the employees that receive them. The value of the shares under the plan cannot exceed 3 million pounds sterling.

Enterprise Union: In Japan, employees of a single company who form a union to represent their interest with management.

Entire Agreement Clause: When included in an agreement, the statement basically says that the agreement between the two parties is contained entirely in the agreement and no other statements or documents can be part of the agreement.

Entity: Although this type of institution has individual members, like a corporation or partnership, it possesses its own existence for legal and tax purposes, and can be treated like an individual if sued, or it can sue as an individual.

Entrepreneur: While the word has various meanings and definitions, some of importance include: person who assumes risk; one who supplies money for new ventures; an innovator or an owner of a new enterprise.

Entry Barriers: Any action or event which would impede a new competitor from entering a market; samples of entry barriers are high investment costs or the need for licenses or government approval.

Environmental Audit: Typically when land is acquired for a business or for public purpose, an environmental due diligence needs to be conducted. In almost all major economies these kinds of audits are part of the planning and building process. The lender also will insist that some kind of environmental inspection be part of any loan package, as the bank will not accept contaminated land, for example, as collateral for a loan.

EOC: *See* ***Equal Opportunities Commission***.

EPA: Acronym in Britain for the Equal Pay Act of 1970 which requires firms to pay men and women the same rate for like or equal employment, including work rates as equivalent or having equal value. Also an acronym for the Environmental Protection Agency (United States).

Equal Opportunities Commission (EOC): An independent group, not government sponsored, which works for eliminating sexual discrimination in all aspects of life and work.

Equitable Distribution: A fair and reasonable distribution of any benefits or gain due a group; dividends from profits, for example.

Equitable Proprietary Interest: A debtor attempts to transfer an asset to the lender as part of the loan obligation, but becomes insolvent before the formalities of the transfer are completed. Nevertheless, the lender will still have an interest in the asset as security to the loan.

Equity of Redemption: Referring to real property, this is the right of a person owing money on a loan or who has a debt on real property to cure his or her default by making the delinquent payments. The process occurs after foreclosure proceedings have commenced.

Equity Investor Loan: Often called mezzanine debt, it is a short-term loan by an equity investor to assist an enterprise, typically to expand its base of business or invest in new technology or research.

ERISA: *See **Employee Retirement Income Security Act**.*

Escalator Clause: A provision in an agreement which allows for an increase in costs (such as an increase in rent payments in a lease) to rise as the cost of living goes up. Most commercial leases have escalator clauses, if for no other reason to protect the owner from future increases in management and insurance costs as well as rising real estate taxes.

Escape Clause: A contractual provision allowing one of the parties to a contract to be excused from any obligations if a certain event within the contract does or does not occur.

Escheat: The abandonment of personal property; for example, property left in safety deposit boxes, unclaimed tax refunds, money left in inactive banking accounts.

Escrow: An account to hold money, legal documents or other assets agreed to by two parties; the arrangement is temporary. Commonly used for property taxes, for example.

Escrow Agent: The individual or entity that holds onto documents and funds in the transfer of real property; this agent often works for both the buyer and seller.

Espionage: In a business context, spying by one company on another with the intent to obtain key confidential information, e.g. pricing policies, new products in development, a key formula or an important new software design. Such actions are illegal.

Essential Industry: Any industry which is protected from outside influence or competition because by its very nature it is sensitive and important for national business and political interests; the defense industry in the United States, for example.

Estate: The total value of one's personal and real property, before taxes or other claims, usually at the time of one's death.

ET1: The standard claim form that is used by an employee to file a discrimination claim against an employer in the United Kingdom.

ET3: A standard form used by the employer to defend itself against an employee claim of discrimination in the United Kingdom.

ETO: see ***economic, technical and organizational***

EURIBOR: Acronym for the Euro Interbank Offered Rate-the rate at which interbank deposit terms are offered by one prime bank to another in the euro zone.

Euro Interbank Offered Rate: *See EURIBOR above.*

European Bank for Reconstruction and Development: *See EBDR.*

European Community Merger Regulation: *See ECMR.*

European Development Fund: *See EDF.*

European Economic Community (EEC): Commonly called the Common Market, it was the product of the Treaty of Rome; it purpose was to break down economic barriers and open a free trade zone within Europe. Since its inception, it has grown dramatically, including its own currency, the euro.

European Monetary System: *See EMS.*

Event of Default: Often specified in commercial loan agreements, these are events which allows the lender to cancel the loan and call for full payment of the amount due. Events of default include non-payment, or late payment or a breach of certain covenants in the loan document.

Evergreen Clause: A right within a contract that allows for some activity automatically, e.g. the right to an automatic extension of a loan or the right to renew a contract when desired.

Exceptions: Deviating from the standard and expected. Something that does not conform to the general rule or procedure in law or business.

Exchange: The process by which people barter for, or trade, property, goods and/or services instead of those goods being purchased via a sale by money.

Exchange Rate: Based on changing market conditions, it is the price at which one country's currency can be changed for another currency. Whole financial markets have been built around this simple concept. Contracts and other international business dealings are at risk because of exchange rate volatility unless some consideration is included.

Exchange Controls: Governmental controls which in effect put limits on the use of foreign exchange; efforts to limit the outflow of hard currency, for example. Businesses find that they cannot meet contractual obligations for the lack of hard currency.

Exchequer: The official account of the Chancellor of the Exchequer of the United Kingdom; it is the account into which gross revenues of the United Kingdom are kept and the account from which expenditures are drawn.

Excise: A tax levied upon the sale, manufacture or consumption of certain goods (e.g. tobacco), as well as a tax on a business license or charter.

Exclusive License: The process by which a copyright owner provides an individual or entity (a licensee) with the ability to exercise an exclusive right, via a valid contract, that belongs to the copyright owner by law. Often this licensee becomes the copyright owner. One party sells another the right to produce a movie in French based on a work or another version of the same movie.

Exclusivity Agreement: An agreement not to shop the terms (sale of a company) to other potential buyers; these kinds of agreements are used to ensure that the other party negotiates solely with the originator for a period of time. In theory they offer protection from being outbid by a third party.

Execute: When dealing with contracts, this term refers to fulfilling one's obligations under a contract. It also refers to fulfilling one's obligations under a court order.

Executor: An individual or company appointed in a will to carry out the provisions of the will, but only upon the death of the will writer. A person who dies without a will is said to be intestate, and the executor typically becomes the state in which he or she lives (in the United States).

Exemption: When dealing with taxation, this refers to a credit given (e.g.

for dependants, disability, etc.) that results in a descending calculation in tax levels.

Exempt Property In a bankruptcy, these are the possessions an individual can keep if he or she loses a lawsuit to a creditor or files for Chapter 7 bankruptcy.

Ex Gratia: Given or provided as a favor, where payment is not required or expected to be made, as in a legal obligation.

EX-IM BANK: *See* ***Export-Import Bank***.

Exit: Often going public, it is one of several means for investors in a private company to get a return on their initial investment. Selling to another private company could also be an exit as well as an employee buyout.

Exit/Reentry Visa: A government permit allowing a foreign national to leave a country and reenter at a later time.

Expense: In business, an immediate, current cost of operation (e.g., payroll, operational bills).

Expenses: Often born by an employee out-of-pocket, these are costs related to and incurred in the normal course of business activities. These costs are usually associated with travel, meals and other expenditures and usually are reimbursed by the employer. An employment contract or an employee manual will bind the employer to pay such expenses which were incurred to the benefit of the company.

Expert Adviser: An independent expert who advises on technical, professional or financial matters-a computer consultant, for example.

Expert Determination: A means of alternative dispute resolution, it is a binding process that can offer relief in settling technical issues or disputes between contracting parties. Naturally, the intent is to avoid litigation and the costs associated with litigation. Language would be included in a contract to cover this contingency; it would never be automatically assumed that this might be a course of action in a dispute.

Expert Witness: A court witness who provides technical or professional knowledge or expertise, say medical, financial or technological.

Export Controls: Governmental limitations on what can and cannot be exported freely. Often imposed on military, scientific or technical information which may be sensitive to national security or to highly competitive businesses. More recently, an imposition in an effort to control terrorism.

Export-Import Bank (EX-IM BANK): In the United States, a government agency whose role is to support American exports to the rest of the world by assisting in credit risk protection and funding export programs.

Export Insurance: Efforts by a manufacturer who is selling in another country to ensure that payment will be made. Such insurance may be extremely important if the exporter's experience in the past has not been good or there is financial or political upheaval in the receiving country.

Export Quota: Government imposed restrictions limiting the volume, value or the kinds of goods/services that may be exported to another country. This is often used to assist a domestic business or industry and may be interpreted as a restraint of trade.

Export Subsidies: Governmental benefits paid to exporting companies, such as tax credits. Generally such subsidies are considered illegal, distorting fair and open trade internationally.

Express Contact: A contract where all the elements that make up a contract (i.e., offer, acceptance, consideration) are written or stated specifically, with clearly laid-out terms.

Express Warranty: A seller makes assurances to the buyer of goods regarding the quality, condition and/or performance of the goods bought. Often this type of warranty comes from the manufacturer of the goods, and it is best to get these warranties in writing.

Expropriation: Seizing or holding property by a foreign government without payment to the owner; expropriation of oil fields and refineries, for example.

Extended Coverage: Purchasing additional or unusual insurance protection, after the warranty has expired, on a new car for example. Also, for unusual circumstances: flood or hurricane insurance, which is not included in the typical insurance policy sold to businesses or consumers.

Extortion: A crime perpetrated when one obtains money or property through threats, intimidation or false claims. Blackmail is a form of extortion.

Extortionate Credit Bargain: Credit is granted or a loan is given at rates that are grossly above the normal interest rates or ordinary lending terms. Interest rates often are controlled by local governing bodies to protect consumers.

Extra-statutory Concession: A taxpayer (consumer or business) is given tax relief or some form of tax concession, even though he is not entitled to it by a strict interpretation of the tax code.

F

401(k) plan: Often provided by an employer, this savings plan, with deferred compensation, allows an employee to set aside a portion of his or her salary/wages for investment and tax savings. The money is invested, at the employee's option, in various types of funds (savings accounts, money markets, bonds, mutual funds, etc.); many employers provide matching funds at a predetermined point in which the employee's plan vests.

Face Amount: Absent any calculation of interest, this is the original amount that is due on a promissory note or an insurance policy, and this amount is written on the document itself.

Face Value: This represents the original cost, written on a certificate, of shares, or also called par value.

Facilitating Intermediary: Any group or entity that makes shipping arrangements or actually ships good to international destinations on behalf of others. The service often includes document processing and customs clearance.

Facilities Management: An outside service provider manages a company's software, hardware and data processing functions, either on site or at a remote location. Increasingly this function is taken off shore to India or the Philippines, for example, as a means to reduce operating costs.

Factor: A term used when a salesperson sells on behalf of others, but in his or her own name, for a commission on the services. Also the sale of receivables to another party, usually at a discount of face value of the receivables. The factor assumes all collection risks.

Failure of Consideration: One party to a contract fails to deliver goods or services promised to the other party, either by refusal or inability (e.g., goods are damaged or worthless)-allowing the party to whom the goods or services were promised to withhold payment, to bring an action before the courts or to require the failing party to perform.

Fair Debt Collection Practices Act (FDCPA): This is a federal law in the United States that prohibits debt collectors (hired by collection agencies) from retrieving a debt by practicing unfair collection practices (e.g., making false claims, harassing people in debt, calling late at night). The Federal Trade Commission is the contact source for debtors with a complaint under this law.

Fair Labor Standards Act (FLSA): A law in the United States that defines the forty-hour workweek, overtime requirements, the federal minimum wage and child labor restrictions, and which makes sure that workers' rights to be paid in a fair manner are adhered too.

Fair Market Value: This represents the price a seller would most likely receive on the open market for property put up for sale.

Fair Trade Laws: These are state laws that have allowed manufacturers or producers of products to set minimum rates for the resale of their products. Many of these laws have been disputed or repealed in some states.

Fair Use: A law that allows for the noncompetitive use of copyrighted material without having to compensate the author or get her permission to use the material. This law also helps remove the author's right to sue for infringement. Often, the fair use of materials is for scholarly purposes or for informing the public.

Fair Value: An arm's length negotiated price between a willing buyer and a willing seller, both acting on their own behalf and for their own interests.

False Advertising: Intentionally misleading a customer or consumer about the quality, price, usefulness or availability of a product. The advertiser may be legally liable for his false statements or promises.

False Pretenses: A fraudulent activity in which the perpetrator makes untrue statements in order to obtain property or money. An example would be claiming that a coin collection is rare when in fact it is a fake collection.

False Statement Acts: Generally found in most contemporary societies, an omnibus act that makes it illegal to misrepresent the facts when securing (buying) personal property, a payment of cash or for applying for credit, such as a bank loan.

Family and Medical Leave Act (FMLA): A federal law that requires employers (with fifty or more employees) to provide employees with up to 12 weeks of unpaid leave in order to attend to certain types of family needs. This leave can be taken within the course of a year and the typical reasons for taking the leave are the birth of a child, adoption of a child, personal illness or the severe illness of a close family member.

FASB: *See* ***Financial Accounting Standards Board.***

Fast Track: Concerning resolution of disputes between two parties in the United Kingdom, it is the process of settling small and straightforward cases below the level of 15,000 pounds sterling. In the United States, this is called Small Claims Court.

FATF: *See* ***Financial Action Task Force.***

FBPs: *See* ***further and better particulars.***

FDCPA: *See* ***Fair Debt Collection Practices Act.***

FDIC: *See* ***Federal Deposit Insurance Corporation.***

Federal Courts: These are the courts brought forth and given jurisdiction by the U.S. Constitution and federal statues to handle civil and criminal actions that fall under the federal purview.

Federal Open Market Committee: Composed of seven members of the board of governors and five members of the Federal Reserve Bank, this committee is most frequently know for the control of the economy by adjusting interest rates and increasing or decreasing liquidity in the marketplace. Their actions directly affect the course of business not only in the United States, but increasingly worldwide.

Federal Question: A basis for filing a civil claim in federal court, these questions arise and are based on topics when a federal question is involved or when the issue is something listed within the U.S. Constitution.

Federal Deposit Insurance Corporation (FDIC): The overall goal is to protect the assets of depositors in federally insured banks. There are limits, which are adjusted periodically, as to how much money in any one bank would be covered in the event of a bank failure.

Federal Trade Commission (FTC): An agency of the U.S. federal government, it is responsible for enforcing antitrust law violations and regulating and investigating unfair or duplicitous business practices

Fee Simple: Private ownership of real estate in which the owner has complete rights, to control, use, sell or otherwise dispose of the property.

Feu: A type of ownership in Scotland whereby the owner has the equivalent of a freehold subject to any annual feu duties.

Fiduciary: A Latin phrase meaning trust, this is often an individual or business placed in a position of trust, and is allowed to act for another because of this trust. Usually a great deal of confidence is placed upon an individual or entity that bears the title of fiduciary.

Financial Accounting Standards Board (FASB): A non-governmental organization for establishing financial standards and reporting regulations in the United States. They are recognized as official and authoritative by the Securities and Exchange Commission (SEC).

Financial Action Task Force (FATF): An inter-governmental body which works to prevent money laundering. The goal is to create policies to ensure that banks and financial institutions are not being used for money laundering and to get banks to accept a common set of standards.

Financial Assets: Instruments or securities which represent intangible assets or which represents a claim to future cash. The claim by the holder can either be fixed or variable, depending upon the nature of the instrument held.

Financial Intermediary: A bank, for example, which acts as an intermediary between lenders (depositors) and borrowers. They are the major source of indirect borrowing.

Financial Ombudsman: An independent service whose goal is to settle disputes between financial institutions and consumers. One role is to ensure that consumers are compensated when they suffer financial loss as a result of the actions of a regulated financial institution. This has nothing to do with ordinary market losses or risk taking.

Financial Services Authority (FSA): A non-government body whose role is to regulate the financial services industry in the United Kingdom. Overall, it is designed to maintain market confidence, promote public awareness, protect consumers and reduce financial crime.

Finder's Fee: A rather general business term referring to compensation to a third party for facilitating a deal or contract. It may be a fixed sum or a percentage of the sale; it is a commission for bringing two parties together to do business as defined under some form of binding contract.

Fiqh: Islamic jurisprudence or the science of the Sharia.

Firm Offer: Under contract law, this refers to an offer, often in writing, which, when made, states that it may not be revoked, withdrawn or amended for the period of time laid out within the offer, and if the offer is accepted it becomes a binding, enforceable contract.

First Closing Date: When takeovers in the United Kingdom occur, this is the date on which the offer document specifies that the offer will cease to be open for acceptance-unless the date is otherwise extended by agreement.

First Lien: The first claim or rights against a property, a mortgage for example.

First World: As opposed to the third world, those countries with highly established economies and a very high standard of living. Most of Europe, North America, Japan, Australia, among others, are first world countries.

Fiscal Year: An accounting year, as opposed to the calendar year. A company's fiscal year may or may not be the same as the calendar year.

Fixed in a Tangible Medium of Expression: This is a requirement that for a work to be protected under copyright law it must exist in a physical form (e.g., a tape, disk, writing, etc.) and cannot simply be spontaneous speech.

Fixed Pay: A basic salary or the pre-determined amount of money payable to an employee.

Fixed Price: A contractual obligation to sell at a stated price regardless of the cost of manufacturing or production.

Fixed Share Partner: Entitled to a fixed portion of the partnership's profits, and depending upon the nature of the agreement, this partner may not have to contribute to partnership losses. Often they have limited voting rights.

Fixture: These are pieces of equipment that have become attached to land, a building or a dwelling in such a fashion that it has become a part of the land, building or a dwelling and its removal would in some way adversely affect the land, building or a dwelling. Often, this deals with equipment that is wired, bolted, nailed, or screwed into a wall, ceiling or floor.

Flexible Working: Any work pattern that deviates from the local, standard norms and hours. This might include flextime, working at home, job sharing, shift work, staggered hours or even part-time work. Flexible working is increasingly becoming popular in the work place.

Flat Rate: No flexibility in pricing, as defined in a contract; the price remains the same regardless of quantity purchased or the price is fixed regardless of the man hours required to do the work.

Flextime: An employment system whereby workers can set their own work shifts-generally implemented within certain parameters. Considered to be a benefit to both employee (improved morale and productivity) and employer (cost savings, better utilization of company facilities).

Float: Money in a deposited in a bank waiting for collection by others; the time between when money is deposited and the time it is withdrawn by the recipient of a check. An extreme form is kiting, which is illegal.

Floatation: When company shares are officially listed on a registered investment exchange, for example the London Stock Exchange.

FLSA: *See* ***Fair Labor Standards Act.***

FMLA: *See* ***Family and Medical Leave Act.***

FOB: *See free on board.*

For Value Received: A term used (when dealing with a promissory note, bill of exchange or deed) to denote that a certain amount of consideration has been provided without actually professing what the payment was.

Forbearance: An agreement, by a debtor and creditor or both parties to a contract, to delay the collection of a debt or in demanding performance on a contract. This delay is usually for a specified period of time. An example would be a borrower of a student loan asking the lender of the loan to halt payment requirements for a stated period, although interest will continue to accrue.

Foreclosure: When the conditions of a mortgage have been violated, the mortgage holder can force the sale of the real property in order to enforce payment of principal, interest, penalties and fees or all of the above.

Forced Sale: This is a sale of goods that were seized in order to fulfill the requirements of a judgment, typically for a failure to perform based on the conditions of a valid contract or mortgage.

Force Majeure: Any series of events which are outside of the control of the parties in an agreement; war and natural disasters are examples. Contracts typically have a force majeure statement to prevent a party from defaulting because of something that it cannot control.

Foreign Corporation: This is a corporation that is incorporated under the laws of another country or of a different state in which it does its business. This type of corporation must files papers with the state it is doing substantial business in to provide it with notice of its operations, as well as name an agent that can accept service within the state.

Foreign Corruption Practices Act: A United States law forbidding bribery, kickbacks and other generally corrupt practices in dealings with foreign officials or business clients. Accounting systems and internal controls must be maintained to ensure that no effort has been made to cover up such practices.

Foreign Subsidiary: A business unit that is part of a larger corporation, but it is incorporated in a foreign country.

Forfeiture: Return of goods for failure to pay; one can also forfeit rights based on an unwillingness or failure to perform certain actions. In the United Kingdom it can also be the commencement of proceedings for possession of rental property by a landlord for non-payment.

Forgery: Counterfeiting, altering or any deliberate attempt to change a document with the intention of defrauding a third party. To make a false document look genuine, as in a forged check.

Form 42: In the United Kingdom, an annual tax information form used by employers to report to the tax authorities about shares or options to shares acquired by employees in that year.

Forthwith: When found in contracts, this means as soon as it can be reasonably done, as it implies immediacy to the other party.

Forum non Conveniens: A Latin term for an inappropriate form as well as the legal doctrine used by common law courts to determine which court has jurisdiction over a claim.

Forward Contract: A cash contract by which the seller agrees to deliver an asset to the buyer at some future date; often used in foreign exchange, for example, to reduce currency fluctuation risks.

Forwarding Agent: Any business or individual who is responsible for transferring, warehousing or delivering goods; for example, a freight forwarder, either interstate or internationally.

Four Corners of an Instrument: This refers to the study of an entire document to understand its meaning, and doing so without utilizing any outside materials or extrinsic evidence. Often a document should be read and taken as whole within its four corners, unless any ambiguous language cannot be understood without outside research.

Four Cs: From a lender's perceptive, vis-à-vis a borrower, they are capital, character, collateral and capacity. The best loan prospects are those with the highest ratings in all four characteristics.

Franchise: In business, this is a license bought by a retailer or supplier which allows him or her to operate a business or sell the goods or services of a particular company under the company's trading name (e.g., McDonalds).

Franchise Tax: A tax levied by a state upon businesses or corporations for the right to do business.

Fraud: For fraud to be present, the activity must be a conscious effort to deceive or falsify. Misappropriation of company assets or manipulation of financial data are examples of corporate fraud.

Freehold: Land ownership that gives absolute ownership of the land and the land's rights.

Free on Board (FOB): This designation refers to goods purchased and transported without charge to a specific location. If a document reads, free on board at the place of manufacture, there will be a charge for delivery to other destinations. For example, if widgets are manufactured in New York and are sold, FOB New York, then a shipping charge will not be applied if purchased and transported anywhere in New York; delivery will be charged if transported to California.

Free of Duty: Free of tariffs or taxes when goods (or services) cross borders. Tariffs can be both protective and income-generating.

Freehold: Typically an estate held for free or for life.

Freeze: As ordered by a government, fixing prices or wages at their current level. A temporary means of controlling inflation, for example.

Freezing Order: This is a court order preventing the disposal of any assets by a defendant pending the resolution of some legal action.

Frictional Unemployment: In a full-employment economy, zero unemployment is never possible. There are always individuals who are between jobs or have re-entered the job market. They are classified as frictionally unemployed.

FRI Lease: A lease whereby the tenant is responsible for all the repairs and insurance.

Frolic: An employee, while working for an employer, deviates from his or her business duties and goes beyond the scope of his or her employment (e.g., visiting a girlfriend while working). If injuries to another or an employee occur while an employee is outside the scope of his or her employment, the employer most likely will not be held liable for any injuries.

Frozen Account: A bank or securities account seized by a court-ordered lien to ensure payment of a judgment, claim or other right. Preventing money from being moved out of the country.

Frustration of Purpose: An unexpected event which when it occurs it makes it impossible for a contract to be performed. This allows the frustrated party to rescind the contract without having to pay damages to the other contracted party. This is also referred to as commercial frustration.

FSA: *See **Financial Services Authority**.*

FTC: *See **Federal Trade Commission***

FTSE 100: An index of the 100 largest companies by market capitalization traded on the London Stock Exchange. There are also FTSE 250 and FTSE 350 indices as well.

Full Disclosure: This refers to the requirement in business transactions that all relevant, known facts and truths be put forward and provided to a buyer or party to a contract. In many states, when dealing with real estate sales, a full disclosure form must be read, filled out and signed, agreeing that, under penalty of perjury, no knowingly false or concealed facts have been presented

Functional Director: A director or manager who has specific responsibility for a particular department, e.g. sales, marketing, human resources or legal.

Fungible Things: Also referred to as fungibles, these are goods which are interchangeable and each is deemed as good as another. They are often sold or delivered as bulk items; examples are: wheat, gravel and identical securities.

Further and Better Particulars (FBPs): A party to a claim can request additional information about the other party's position or defense. If there is no response within 7 days, the originating party can request the court or tribunal that the request be honored.

G

G8: Acronym for Group of Eight-an international forum of the governments of Canada, France, Germany, Italy, Japan, Russia, United Kingdom and the United States. Together, they represent approximately 65 percent of the world's gross national product. Although an informal summit, the group meets regulary to discuss the world economy, terrorism and the environment, among other topics.

GAAP: *See* ***generally accepted accounting principles.***

GAAS: *See* ***generally accepted auditing standards.***

GAAT: *See* ***General Agreement on Tariffs and Trade.***

Gains: Any increase in equity (net assets) as a result of deliberate or non-deliberate acts of an enterprise. Selling more goods or winning a lawsuit are both examples of gains.

Gap Analysis: In business, the difference in sales between what was budgeted and the actual sales levels for a period (quarter, year). The original budget may have been unrealistic or sales were less because of competition, obsolescence of the product line or because of an ineffective corporate operation. The gap may result in contractual conflict or other kind of legal exposure.

Garden (Gardening) Leave: In the United Kingdom this kind of leave is often used when an employee gives notice. While the employee is still on staff and under contract, the employer does not want the employee to attend to office functions or contact customers. The employer's concern is that the employee is leaving for a competitor and does not want to allow any opportunity for the terminating employee to gain some advantage for his new employer.

Garnishment: A creditor obtains a court order directing an individual or entity to hold onto money they owe an individual, because the individual is in debt to another person or entity.

Gazette Notice: An offer of securities is made to overseas shareholders using an advertisement in the *London Gazette*, as required by the Companies Act of 1985.

Geared Leases: A grant by an owner of property in the United Kingdom whereby a long lease (say 125 years) to a developer or investor, who in turn, will lease or rent portions of the property to others. Geared leases are often made at a premium, if for no other reason, the length of time involved.

Gearing: Similar to the concept of leverage, meaning the ratio of debt to owners' equity in a firm. It is a measure of risk, meaning the higher the percentage of debt, the greater the risk because a highly-geared company has a large debt burden which must be paid no matter the level of sales or the profitability of the company. Such companies are at risk legally and financially, as they may not be able to fulfill contractual agreements or loan covenants.

Gender Bias: A situation where an employer, based on the sex of an employee or group of employees, offers unequal treatment to these individuals with regard to employment opportunities (e.g., pay, promotions, bonuses, etc.); often this treatment can lead to lawsuits under antidiscrimination laws.

General Agreement on Tariffs and Trade (GATT): A free-trade treaty aimed at promoting global economic growth. To accomplish its goals, GATT promotes the idea that by negotiations on trade policies and tariff reductions it can encourage free trade among countries, with part of its guidelines requiring members to offer copyright protections to authors of member countries. GATT was signed in 1947 by most developed nations.

General Counsel: Employed by corporations, and often the chief legal counsel for the corporation, these individuals are often paid as full-time, salaried employees, for legal services provided to the corporation. The term house counsel also designates an attorney that works for only one business.

General Partner: Often one of the owners of a partnership, which is a joint business for profit. A general partner, in contrast to the owners of a corporation, can be held personally liable for business debts and obligations, but may also take actions and bind the business (e.g., sign contracts), which would in turn also bind the other partners.

General Prohibition: The Financial Services and Markets Act 2000 says that no person can carry on a regulated activity (financial) unless he is authorized (licensed) to do so.

Generally Accepted Accounting Principles (GAAP): Those conventions, rules or procedures as prescribed by an accounting authority on how various transactions and accounting practices must be handled. A company is in conformity when it follows GAAP.

Generally Accepted Auditing Standards (GAAS): The professional responsibilities and standards that an auditor must follow when reviewing a company's books.

Genuine Occupational Qualification or Requirement: Setting the issue of discrimination aside, there are times when a person of a specific race or religion is required to perform a job-a rabbi must be Jewish to perform the duties of a rabbi.

Ghara: This is prohibited in Islamic finance; it does not allow for uncertainty in a contract. A party stands to be deceived because they do not know the future outcome; gambling and financial speculation are examples.

Gift *Causa Mortis*: A gift made in the expectation of imminent death (on the condition that the donor dies).

Gilt-edged Securities (Gilts): Government bonds from the United Kingdom-a form of long-term government borrowing with a fixed term and a standard rate of interest paid to the bond holders. They are for the conservative investor and are considered rock-solid securities, with no risk of default.

Giro System: Started in Germany and used throughout Europe, it is an account which facilitates the movement of funds from debtors by order of the debtor directly to the bank.

GmBH: Gesellschaft mit beschrAnkter Haftug. In Germany, this is a designation of a form of limited liability company.

Go-between: A generic term for one who acts on behalf of another; a broker or intermediary, for example. In labor negotiations, a go-between mediates between labor and management.

Going Concern: An enterprise that is operating as opposed to one that has temporarily stopped trading, closed down or is in the process of being liquidated.

Golden Formula: In the United Kingdom, when a trade union is organizing an industrial action, it can incur civil liability unless its activities fall within the golden formula, i.e. its actions are only done in furtherance of a labor dispute.

Golden Handshake: Often called a golden parachute, extraordinary benefits (financial and otherwise) granted to senior managers or directors leaving their employer, either through termination or retirement. Increasingly, there is public outcry on the part of investors when such arrangements are excessive; many feel that directors fail in their fiduciary responsibility by approving such arrangements.

Golden Parachute: Controversial and extravagant benefits package awarded a senior manager or director at the end of his employment; often used if a company is a takeover candidate. Shareholders are increasingly militant about this kind of management compensation. *See* ***golden handshake*** *above*.

Good Faith: The honest intent to act in a fair and equitable manner without taking unfair advantage over another individual, or to fulfill agreed upon promises to act, even though it appears that a particular legal technicality would not be fulfilled.

Good Leaver/Bad Leaver: When an employee leaves an employer, a good leaver is one who terminates because for legitimate reasons (even death or disability) while a bad leaver is dismissed for cause.

Good Title: Ownership in real or personal property which can be shown is owned free and clear, without limitation or encumbrance.

Goods: Various items for sale and held by a business in the normal course of business, such as items in a retail store.

Goodwill: This is a non-tangible benefit that a business builds over time, such as having a good reputation with clients, customers, etc. This represents the value of the business beyond its physical assets, and often is represented when the business is sold, as it can have a positive impact of the overall value of the business. Sellers prefer that the goodwill be high since it is not subject to capital gains taxes and represents more profit in the sale of the business, while buyers prefer it be low because it cannot be depreciated like tangible assets.

Government Regulation: An increasing tendency by governments to be involved in the daily business and social practices of society. Regulation can be both positive (prevention of fraud or monopolies) and negative (restricting trade unnecessarily to protect domestic producers). Generally, it is a huge network of rules and regulation, at times contradictory and almost always complex. Government regulation, by definition, is a major cost center for most companies.

Governmental Immunity: From English common law, this provided that no governmental body could be sued unless it gives its permission. Often providing unjust results, this rule has been negated under the Federal Tort Claims Act and state waivers of immunity.

GP: *See* ***grievance procedure***.

Grace Period: Under the law of contracts, this a time provided for in a contract that allows for performance or a late payment to be made without penalty. Often after this period ends-and if the late payment or performance has not been received-the contract is suspended.

Graft: Using a business or government position for personal or financial benefit; taking a cash payoff or other non-cash remuneration, such as free vacations, trips or expensive gifts. An illegal act in every jurisdiction.

Grandfather Clause: Often found in statutes or zoning ordinances, this is a clause that allows a business or land owner to continue to operate his or her business or use his or her land as it is, and they will be exempt from any restrictions on use, as long as they continue to operate the business or use the land in the same way as when the law was put into place. If, however, the business or land use begin to be utilized for other purposes then the grandfather clause will no longer protect the owner. For example, an ordinance is passed which excludes retail businesses from operating in a zone, but if that type of business already operates in that zone it can continue to operate as is, even if it has new owners; if it changes from a retail establishment the clause will lapse.

Grantor: Being a donor or granting another a benefit.

Gratuity: A gift or donation; if given for a purpose, say to influence another, it often is either illegal or unethical. Many organizations limit the kinds and amounts of gratuities officers and managers may receive.

Greenmail: Where enough shares have been bought by an entity or individual to allow for a hostile takeover of a company, and the entity or individual can then force the company that can be taken over into purchasing back the shares at a higher price in order to stave off the possibly of a takeover.

Grey Market Trading: A situation whereby importers bring branded goods into the local market from other locations where they are bought more cheaply.

Grievance Procedure (GP): A procedure for employers to deal with grievances, real or imagined, by employees as is mandated in the Employment Act 2002 in the United Kingdom.

Gross Income: Utilized in calculating income tax, this is the income an individual or business gets from all sources, but before any deductions have been taken, because when taken these result in the net income.

Ground Floor: An asset acquired for a very low price, which has the potential to or subsequently does gain in value. An investor in an initial public offering (IPO) which has grown substantially in value is said to have invested on the ground floor.

Guarantor: An individual or entity that agrees to be held accountable for the nonpayment or nonperformance on a debt or to a contract that is made by another.

Guaranty: Something given as security for performance; also, an assurance to a consumer that the product or service is as expected and that in the event of defect, repairs or replacement will be provided.

Guardian ad Litem: A court-appointed representative to manage the interests of a minor in a lawsuit.

H

Hak Tamalluk: Ownership rights under Islamic law.

Halifax House Price Index: It is the authoritative report on housing prices in the United Kingdom. Published by the Halifax and Bank of Scotland, it is a monthly report used by almost all interested parties: the government, the media and businesses.

Haram: Something which is illegal or forbidden under the Koran.

Harassment: Sexual, for example; any words, gestures, threats, policies or actions by an employer or by a supervisor which causes substantial emotional distress to an individual. Harassment could be applied/based on age, minority status, handicap; it can also be interpreted as to influencing another individual during a civil or criminal proceeding.

Hardship Allowance: Additional pay and benefits paid to employees of government agencies or multinational businesses for service in countries where the working conditions are hazardous, risky or unpleasant. Such allowances may be paid during war or where living conditions are below standard.

Hart-Scott-Rodino: Parties to large stock transactions must notify the antitrust Division of the U. S. Department of Justice and the U. S. Federal Trade Commission in order that transactions are reviewed to see if a full-fledged investigation is warranted.

Hawala: Under Islamic practice, a bill of exchange or a remittance, used for settling international debt by book transfers rather than actual cash payments.

Heads of Terms: Simply a term sheet or a memorandum of understanding which sets out the terms of a commercial transaction which the parties have agreed to in principle in the course of their negotiations. While heads of terms have moral imperative, they are not legally binding on either party.

Hearsay: A written or oral statement which is not first-hand evidence, and thus has no merit in a court of law.

Hedge Clause: Written into a contract or general agreement, it is a statement where one party repudiates any responsibility for the accuracy of information from sources beyond his control which were used in the creation of the contract-using industry or consumer data that may or may not be accurate as an estimate of sales, for instance.

Heir: Any person who is a successor to real property by operation of the law or through a will. An heir-at-law to an estate from a deceased person.

Hetarchy: In business, a management structure whereby all officers are of equal rank; there is no hierarchical structure. A joint venture, where all companies to the venture are equal.

HIDC: *See* ***holder is due course.***

Hidden Asset: An item that is purposefully left off the books of a company, often with the intention of evading taxation on the item or to hide it during bankruptcy proceedings. Although, there are also legitimate reasons to leave items off the books as well.

Hidden Damage: Harm to goods which is not obvious to the buyer; damage done in transit and not known until a product is utilized for its intended purpose.

Hive Down: A company reorganization whereby a business is transferred to a subsidiary.

Hive Up: Transferring assets or a business to the parent company.

HM Revenue & Customs (HMRC): The United Kingdom government department responsible for taxes. It is the result of the merger of Inland Revenue and Customs & Excise.

Hobby Loss: Dealing in the area of income tax, this is a type of loss incurred by an individual or a so-called business that is engaged in an activity that does not seek a profit. Generally, these losses are only deductible from the revenue produced by the hobby.

Holder in Due Course (HIDC): An individual has paid for the right to hold a promissory note or check and, in good faith, believes that it is good and without any claims against it, that is was not previously dishonored or overdue in its payment to another. The HIDC, having taken the document in good faith, is entitled to receive payment on the document from its maker.

Holder: In business terms, this often refers to one who is in possession of a promissory note, bond, check or other paper (through endorsement or delivery), for which he or she is entitled to the payment specified on the note.

Holding Company: Often a corporation, it is formed with the express purpose of purchasing and holding the stocks of other companies. This ownership of stock frequently provides the corporation with managerial control over the other companies.

Holographic Will: A will written in the testator's own handwriting, signed and dated. Not all jurisdictions accept such wills.

Home Leave: Employees of multinational corporations who are stationed overseas are allowed to return home for a period of time at company expense. The stipend may cover the employee as well as her family.

Honor: To pay on a check or demand draft when presented to the bank for payment.

Horizontal Trading Company: A group of companies in the same industry with similar products form an industry group to promote sales and exports, e.g. beef cattle producers.

Hostile Bid: An unwarranted or unwanted attempt to gain control of another company. It may be for the purposes of greenmail or a genuine attempt to own and possibly merge the desired company with another company.

House Counsel: Different from a general counsel, this is a lawyer that works only for a certain type of/particular business.

Human Resource Management (HRM): That part of an organization devoted to the hiring, firing, training, evaluating and compensation of employees at the workplace. From both legal and business points of view, the human resource department has a tremendous responsibility to manage all functions of human resource development not only by company and industry standards, but also according to the laws and regulations governing labor.

Hush Money: A payment or gratuity paid by one party to another for their silence about improper, unethical or illegal behavior of the one paying the hush money.

Hybrid Scheme: A pension scheme (retirement plan) that is neither a pure defined benefit scheme nor a pure defined contribution scheme.

Hypothecate: A Greek term of origin meaning pledge, i.e. where property is used to secure a loan, although the borrower continues to retain possession. This in turn creates a secured debt. An example is a standard mortgage on a piece of property or a building.

I

IAPC: *See* ***International Auditing Practices Committee.***

IASB: *See* ***International Accounting Standards Board.***

ICA: *See* ***International Commodity Agreement.***

ICAEW: *See* ***Institute of Chartered Accountants of England & Wales.***

I & C Agreement: *See* ***information and consultation agreement.***

ICC: *See* ***International Chamber of Commerce.***

ICSC: Acronym for the International Central Securities Depository, a central depository designed to facilitate the transfer and trading of various international securities.

ICSID: Acronym for the International Centre for Settlement of Investment Disputes which was founded in 1966 and is a division of the World Bank. It provides facilities for arbitration of disputes from member countries.

IDB: Acronym for the Inter-American Development Bank, established in 1959, to promote Latin American and Caribbean economic development.

Ijara: While similar to a conventional lease, whereby the financial institution or bank leases an asset to the lessee in return for the agreed payment, the financial institution is willing to take on more of the risk, such as loss or damage of the asset. In effect, the convention conforms to Islamic law.

Ijara wa-Iktina (Finance Lease): The financial institution buys an asset, leases it to a customer for a specific price and period of time and then sells the asset to the customer for the agreed upon price at the end of the lease. This arrangement is structured under Islamic law.

Ijara: While similar to a conventional lease, whereby the financial institution or bank leases an asset to the lessee in return for the agreed payment, the financial institution is willing to take on more of the risk, such as loss or damage of the asset. In effect, this convention conforms to Islamic law.

Ill-health Condition: In order to receive a pension before normal retirement, an individual to a pension scheme must prove that he is unable to continue to work (his normal occupation) because of physical or mental disability. He must show proof from a medical practitioner in order to be awarded an early pension.

Illiquid: Not readily converted to cash; property or fixed assets are often considered illiquid.

Illusory Promise: A promise to an agreement that is so indefinite and unspecified that it can not be ascertained by an individual or entity as to what is to be done; or performance is optional. The other party to the agreement then cannot be held to obligations for payment or performance under such an agreement.

ILO: Acronym for the International Labour Organization, a division within the United Nations, that deals specifically with labor issues. The goal is to promote quality work and working conditions world-wide. It is very active in the elimination of child labor.

IMF: Acronym for the International Monetary Fund, the organization was found in 1945 partially in response to the economic chaos at the end of World War II. Today, the 185 nation voluntary organization's goals are to promote global monetary cooperation, insure financial stability in the capital and banking systems of the world and facilitate world trade. The reduction of poverty has been the standard by which the organization has worked and acted.

Immediately: In contract dealings, this refers to when something must be done, as soon as it can be done, without any excuses as to why it cannot be done.

Impairment: The value of an asset or entity is damaged or reduced by some action on the part of another or because of some event outside of the owner's control.

Implied Contract: An agreement which exists based not necessarily on writing, but rather on certain circumstances and actions by both parties which places a contract between the two in existence. Often, this type of contract arises when it would be detrimental to one party and/or unjustly enrich the other party. This is different from an expressed contract.

Implied Covenant of Good Faith and Fair Dealings: A general law of contracts whereby there is an assumption that parties to a contract will act in good faith towards one another and deal fairly. A breach of this covenant can lead to a lawsuit, and it can be brought when the offending party uses technical excuses for the breach or willfully misconstrues specific words in the contract to refuse his or her obligations.

Implied Term: An item in a contract that is not expressly agreed upon by the two parties, but is implied either because of common law or statute-meaning that the matter is customary and ordinary.

Implied Warranty: This is a presumption that goods and/or services function as they ought to, and are merchantable and can be used by consumers for its intended purpose, unless the consumer purchases the product or services as is, or second-hand without the knowledge of any warranty.

Import: Goods produced in one country and shipped for sale or use to another country.

Import Quotas: Any artificial limit on the quantity of goods or the value of those goods which may be moved from one country to another. The quotas can be imposed voluntarily by producers or by the governments of one or the other countries.

Impossibility: Under contract law, this is when an act cannot be performed due to unforeseen events, natural causes or some type of physical problem. This provides a legitimate out from a contract by both parties through mutual rescission.

In Lieu: Meaning instead. An example is in lieu taxes, which are use taxes that are paid as opposed to sales tax.

***In Pari Delicto*:** Latin term meaning in equal fault. This term in law refers to when two or more people are equally at fault, so, in contractual law, if both parties are comparatively at fault then neither side can claim a breach by the other party.

Incentives: Any additional fee or remuneration given to an individual or business to encourage performance, often above the average. Sales people receive an incentive to increase business.

Income Tax: A tax placed upon one's gross earnings, less any deductions, which results in a net income. The Federal government collects their own income tax, while most states also collect an income tax, although at a lower rate.

Income Withdrawal: In the United Kingdom, owners of a money purchase scheme who are under age 75 can draw an annual income from their unsecured pension while leaving the rest of the money invested. Different plans rules come into play when members reach age 75.

Income: This can be in the form of money, goods, services or other economic benefits received by an individual or entity. Often income is derived from working, but can also be had through stock dividends, rent or other investments or ventures.

Incorporated: A term used in the United States as an indication that a company or concern is a corporation, with all the legal rights and obligations afforded to that status.

Incoterms: International trade terms which have been standardized under the authority of the International Chamber of Commerce (ICC). They cover the liabilities and responsibilities of both buyers and sellers from different countries.

Indemnification: Where an employer, in order to rectify a loss suffered by an employee while working, makes a compensatory payment to that employee.

Indemnify: To provide a guarantee to another against any potential loss that he or she might suffer. For example, where there is a contract dispute between two parties that is settled, one party might offer to pay any future claims that might arise from it, having the effect of holding harmless the other party

Indemnity: An effort by a seller to cover a possible loss by the buyer which is of particular concern; under an indemnity, the seller will reimburse the entire cost of the loss. A buyer has an obligation to a customer to meet a deadline, and if the seller is late in delivering the goods, the buyer wants an indemnity that the goods will be there as stated.

Independent Contractor: An individual or entity that is hired by another to complete a specified job. The details of the job, including duties, pay and other matter, are often listed within the contract between the parties. Independent contractors are not considered statutory employees, and therefore are not under the day-to-day control of an employer.

Independent Scrutineer: During a trade union election in the United Kingdom, for example, a person of competence and independence might be assigned to oversee the balloting to ensure the fairness of the election.

Index Linking: Correlating wages or interest rates, for example, to some standard or index. Wages could be linked to the inflation rate. If inflation for one year is 3 percent, wages would be increased by the same amount the following year to ensure the buying power on the part of the employee.

Individual Voluntary Arrangement (IVA): As a means to avoid bankruptcy, an IVA is an arrangement between an insolvent individual and a creditor whereby they agree to terms. An individual is appointed to oversee the process.

Industrial Espionage: Any attempt to steal or illegally obtain protected information or processes from a company or other entity. Essentially stealing trade secrets for financial gain.

Industrial Training Levy (ITA): In the United Kingdom, the ITA imposes a cost on employers in certain industries to finance an industry training board and to fund the actual training itself. One example is the Construction Industry Training Board (CITB).

Industry Standard: What is a common and expected standard within a particular industry. Often called a benchmark, it could be based on quality, number of units produced or the profitability of similar companies.

Information and Consultation Agreement (I & C Agreement): An agreement between employers and employees for the setting up of national works councils whose purpose is to provide information and consultation to each party-a means of exchanging views and opening dialogue between the parties.

Informed Consent: An agreement, only after all relevant facts are identified and acknowledged, to carry out an act or allow something to happen. Under contractual law, an agreement under a contract may be formed when full disclosure has been provided by both parties regarding knowledge significant to the contract.

Infringement: With regards to patent, trademark and copyright law, this is the improper use by another of a protected invention or creative work without the permission of the owner, or an agreement to pay the owner royalties. Accidental infringement is not a defense, and the accidental user must still pay damages or royalties for improper use.

Inherent Vice: In the insurance industry, a hidden defect in a product that could result in damage to the product. Most insurance policies do not cover inherent vice as the damage does not result from some outside, unforeseen event.

Initial Public Offering (IPO): The first offering of public stock, often by companies emerging from the entrepreneurial stage. For owners and early investors, it is a way of cashing out of a growing company. IPOs often can be speculative.

Injury: Legal recourse is available to an individual or a business because of a violation of some right by another individual or business.

Insider Trading: The illegal use of privileged information attained by working within a company or stock brokerage that aids the individual in buying and selling shares and/or bonds because he or she knows, based on this private information, which direction in value the stocks will go. This is a crime under the Securities and Exchange Act.

INSOL Global Principles for Multi-Creditor Workouts: Standards promulgated by INSOL International (*see below*), these are statements of best practice for international, multi-creditor workouts or restructurings. The best practices have jurisdiction in countries which have developed insolvency laws.

INSOL International: The International Federation of Insolvency

Professionals, an industry association of professionals dealing with bankruptcy and insolvency in an international arena.

Insolvency: Where one's total assets, which might be available to pay debt, are less than the total of one's debts, and therefore there is an inability to pay-off or make payments on the debt(s) when needing to do so.

Insolvency Practitioner: Generally an accountant, an individual licensed by a professional organization and trained specifically in matters of business insolvency. An insolvency practitioner acts as a liquidator or administrator during insolvency proceedings.

Insolvent: Unable to pay debts when due.

Installment Contract: Where it is agreed upon that a series of payments-often based on fixed dates or upon certain happenings-are to be made for delivery of goods, performance of services or payments of money. If there is a failure in payment or in services rendered of one of the installments when due, this is considered a breach of the contract between the parties, and damages for missing the installment may be sought; or this failure may relieve the other party from having to perform their part of the contract.

Institute of Chartered Accountants in England & Wales (ICAEW): A professional accountancy organization in the United Kingdom and Wales, founded in 1880, it has over 128,000 members. Membership in an accountancy society is not a legal requirement in England, and as such this is just one of many overlapping organizations that support the accounting profession.

Instrument: A written document of legal significance, such as a contract, deed, will or bond.

Instrumentality: Literally, an agent, often of a government or governing body. They are corporations but exempt from taxation.

Insurable Interest: For insurance to be valid, the insured must have an interest or ownership on the item insured. Generally, you cannot insure something you do not own-some one else's home, for example.

Insurance: A contract between an individual or entity and an insurer, in which the insurer agrees to pay for all or a portion of the other party's (insured party) loss suffered by accident, negligence or death, in exchange for a fee—often paid bi-annually or monthly.

Insurance Broker: An individual or group practice that sells, arranges or negotiates a variety of insurance needs for both individuals and companies. Insurance brokers need to be licensed by a local governing body and are required to take continuing educational courses. They may sell or broker life, health, property and casualty insurance, for example.

Intangible Property: This is personal property, such as shares in a company, that, while they have no physical existence, they do have value, even though they are not tangible property. Other examples include, patents, copyrights, goodwill and trademarks.

Intercompany Loan: Any borrowing or exchange of money or assets between and among divisions or affiliates of a larger company; because the loans are made within the company, they do not represent new or additional debt by the corporation. The activity is not reflected on the balance sheet.

Intercompany Transactions: Similar treatment for reporting purposes as intercompany loans, these transactions are not recorded on the consolidated financial statements as they have no affect on the totals. They are merely shifts, loans or sales within the company and assets are therefore not depleted or sold when viewed by the larger organization.

Integration: In business and contractual dealings, parties agree to adopt or add a writing to an existing agreement.

Intellectual Property (IP): This is an area of law that deals with patent, copyright and trademark law, and regulates the ownership and use of these types of works. Owners of intellectual property have the right to use or exploit the content for their personal and business purposes without infringement by third parties.

***Inter Se*:** A Latin term meaning, among themselves, and this legal phrase, when used within a corporate environment, might mean, for example, certain corporate rights are designated only to shareholders as a group.

Interchange Agreement: Parties will write an agreement by which they will create and govern the rules concerning electronic data interchange (EDI).

Interconnection: Telecommunications networks communicate with each other and establish rules and procedures to allow communication between and among customers of various networks.

Intercreditor Agreement: A master plan or agreement to regulate the order and respective rights of various creditors during a period of financing. Assume three banks are lenders to a company, an intercreditor agreement would outline who gets paid first in the event of liquidation.

Interest: An amount of money that has accrued and is to be paid by an individual or entity who borrowed money from another, possibly for a loan or to pay a debt. The initial money loaned is the principal, whereas the interest which accrues on the loan is above and beyond the principal money borrowed. The amount and/or percentage of interest to be changed are often stated in writing when the money is loaned. Interest can also accrue (build-up) from money an individual places in a savings account. In this instance, by placing one's money within a bank savings account; the interest that is accruing is paid to the individual that has placed the money into the account above and beyond the principal.

Interest Rate Cap: Under a cap arrangement, the seller of the cap will make payments to the buyer if interest rates go above an agreed rate. In anticipation of this possibility, the buyer will pay the seller a premium for entering into this kind of arrangement, thus a form of interest rate insurance.

Interest Rate Floor: Basically the opposite of an interest rate cap (*see above*) where by the seller, in return for a premium, will pay to the buyer the difference between the specified floor rate and the lower variable rate, should the variable rate fall below that floor.

Interest Rate Risk: One of several business risks encountered in daily business transactions, it is the variability of interest rates and the effect on bonds or other fixed income securities as well as the cost of borrowing money to expand operations or acquire another company.

Interference: When dealing with patent law, this term refers to the process by which conflicts are resolved when two or more patent applications have been filed regarding the same type of invention. This decision is made by the U.S. Patent and Trademark Office after going through a process which involves who first put together and tested the invention, who initially worked out the details of the invention, as well as other factors which are used to determine who owns the patent rights.

Interim Receiver: Meant to protect a debtor's assets, the court may appoint an interim receiver during the bankruptcy process. Either the debtor or the creditor can petition the court for an interim receiver.

Interlineation: A party or both parties to a written agreement write between the lines or in the margins of the document to add something that was thought of at a later date; or to make a correction to something within the document. Problems arise when there is a question as to whether both parties agreed to the added changes or whether the added language was originally part of the document when it was signed. To prevent these types of problems both parties should initial each change or re-write and resign the document.

Intermodal: Transportation of goods or commodities using different means, e.g. truck, train and air freight.

Internal Revenue Service (IRS): In the United States, the IRS is part of the Treasury Department. Its specific role is the collection of taxes and enforcement of federal tax legislation, including processing individual and corporate tax returns and auditing the same.

International Accounting Standards Board (IASB): This is an independent London-based accounting standards board whose role is to smooth out differences in accounting principles and standards used worldwide. The ultimate goal is to get financial reporting around the world to be as consistent as possible.

International Auditing Practices Committee (IAPC): A committee of the International Federation of Accountants (IFA) whose goal is to establish guidelines for generally accepted auditing standards for international application and use.

International Centre for the Settlement of Investment Disputes (ICSID): An international organization whose role is to arbitrate investment treaty disputes. Many of these investment treaties call for arbitration, which ICSID is willing and able to assist in this process.

International Chamber of Commerce (ICC): The goal of this organization is to promote international trade, investment and market economy principles in general. An important role is its services for arbitration for international trade disputes.

International Commodity Agreement (ICA): A formal, written agreement whereby countries who have significant business in the exporting of commodities work toward a smooth operation of the commodities businesses. The ICA assists in setting prices and conducts marketing and research to the benefits of its members.

International Import Certificate: When doing business in the United States, the Department of Commerce requires certain importers to acquire such a certificate to insure that imported goods will be disposed of properly and according to U.S. laws.

International Labor Office: *See ILO.*

International Monetary Fund: *See IMF.*

International Primary Market Association (IPMA): This is the trade association for the major international banks who are underwriters of debt issues for the public sector and debt and equity underwriters for the private (corporate) sector.

International Trade Association (ITA): The goal of the organization is to assist United States companies compete in the world marketplace. It is a division of the Department of Commerce.

International Union: Any union with affiliates in more than one country.

Internet Service Provider (ISP): This is a type of business that provides access to the Internet and Internet services and may, in some circumstances, provide other types of Web-related services. Although protected by the Digital Millennium Copyright Act, there are some instances where this protection lapses and an ISP can be held responsible for subscribers' copyright-infringing material posted on a site.

Interstate Commerce: This concerns commerce regulated by the federal government (Article I of the Constitution), and it includes the movement of goods or money, commercial trade, business, or the transportation of goods from one state to another. Commerce within a state can also be regulated by the federal government if it is commerce that will have an influence on the interstate movement of goods and services ultimately. Currently, although not inclusively, commerce is regulated by the Interstate Commerce Commission (ICC) on the basis of the Interstate Commerce Act, first enacted by Congress in 1887.

Intervention: The central bank or banks buy or sell foreign exchange in order to influence (often to stabilize) a particular currency.

Intestacy: The estate of a person who dies without leaving a will. An administrator is then appointed by a probate court to mange the estate (or liquidate it, as the case may be).

Intimation: In Scotland, a law which is equivalent to a notice of assignment.

Introduction: When a company first seeks to get a listing for its securities on a recognized investment exchange. Typically, a significant number of shares need already have been sold to or in the hands of the public to justify the listing(s).

Invention: Creation of a new product, service or technology which may be exploited for personal or commercial purposes.

Inventory: This is a stock list of the goods that are finished or in production and that are owned and stored by a company. Each list will detail the cost, price and value of said goods.

Inverse Condemnation: Where a government agency has taken property and damaged it so badly that the entire real property has suffered what is equivalent to a condemnation of the property as a whole. In this instance, the property owner seeks payment and will argue he is entitled to compensation under the constitution for condemnation of property by the government under the eminent domain right.

Invest: To place money into a business or to buy property or securities with the anticipation that these investments will turn a profit

Investment Company: Any company, by its own definition, that is in the business primarily to invest, reinvest or trade securities. The American investment company was loosely based on the British investment trust (*see above*).

Investment Media: The general classes or types of property in which capital is invested for gain, when for increase in principal, current gain, or both. A sampling is as follows: savings bonds, time deposits, savings accounts, government bonds, bills, notes and obligations, municipal and state obligations, insurance, annuities, commodities, precious metals and jewels, art objects, real estate, corporate stocks, bonds and warrants, as well as foreign exchange, among others.

Investment Property Databank Index (IPD Index): An index which tracks actual property transactions from institutional investors and property companies. This index includes retail, office and industrial properties.

Investment Services Directive (ISD): One of the European Union directives, it establishes the conditions under which licensed investment firms and banks can provide services in E.U. member countries. Such services might include underwriting, brokerage or portfolio management, among others.

Investor: A person hired by an individual to make investments on their behalf, or an individual that makes the investments for their own gain (for herself or himself).

Investor Protection Committees (IPCs): In the United Kingdom, large institutional investors may be members of organizations such as the Association of British Insurers. The IPCs issue guidelines which most institutions then follow voluntarily, such as on issuing new shares.

Invisible Hand: Concept accredited to Adam Smith in *The Wealth of Nations* stating that people will act in such a way as to benefit themselves; at the same time, he is lead by an invisible hand which means that his actions also promote the general good.

Invisible Imports: The non-tangible, often financial and ancillary aspects of importing; all the items other than the merchandise itself-cost of transportation, interest charges, travel expenses, and so forth.

Invitee: An individual that has come onto another's property or business upon an invitation. Often for business purposes the invitation is implied, like when a store is open, but the invitation can also be direct. In each instance an invitee can assume that the premises is safe, and any injuries not occurring out of the invitee's own negligence or as a result of an unsafe, non-obvious condition, while on the premises, may subject the owner to liability for any injuries suffered.

Invoice: A written document that lays out and summarizes the costs associated with a business transaction and lists the goods or services that have been ordered, along with other pertinent information-it often includes a payment request as well.

IP: See ***intellectual property***.

IPC: See ***Investor Protection Committee***.

IPD Index: See ***investment property databank index***.

IPMA: See ***International Primary Market Association***.

IPO: See ***initial public offering***.

Irish Dividend: A humorous expression about the quality of a stock. Instead of receiving a dividend, the holder is called upon to pay an assessment. Basically, a bad stock.

Irrevocable Credits: Amending or revoking credits can only be done with the assent to all parties to an agreement: the buyer, the seller and the bank.

Irrevocable Letter of Credit: A letter of credit that, if all the terms and conditions are met by the bearer, a specific payment is guaranteed by the bank.

IRS: See ***Internal Revenue Service***

ISD: See ***investment services directive***.

ISDA Master Agreement: In the financial markets, this is the most widely-used form of documentation for derivative transactions and trading. The document can be used for most derivative transactions.

ISP: See ***internet service provider***.

Issue: When dealing with business finances, this refers to the number of shares or bonds of a corporation that have been sold or distributed.

Istijrar: Under Islamic law, this is a recurring sale, different or the same quantities from the same seller over time.

Istisna'a (Construction or Manufacturing Financing): Under Islamic law, the financial institution funds a supplier to create a specific item and thus acquires title to the product. The financier then sells or leases the inventory/product to the supplier.

ITA: See ***industrial training levy.***

IVA: *See* ***individual voluntary arrangement***.

ITO: Acronym for the International Trade Organization, organized in 1944 as a complement to the World Bank and the International Monetary Fund, the organization's main goal was to reduce tariffs and thus promote trade worldwide. Its most significant document is the General Agreement on Tariffs and Trade (GATT) which continues to define trading and tariff arrangements world wide.

Ittifaq Dhimni: Under Islamic law, a pre-agreed contract; prices are agreed prior to contract.

J

Jawboning: In an effort to contain inflation and maintain labor peace, informal pressure is put on labor leaders by government officials to keep demands reasonable during master labor agreement contract negotiation.

JMLSG: *See* ***joint money laundering steering group***.

Job Classification: Almost all larger companies worldwide differentiate between and among employment responsibilities, creating categories based on the kind of work to be done, compensation, whether management or not; also a means for analysis for productivity and other business purposes. Classifications may result in binding labor contracts which reflect various levels of responsibility.

Job Descriptions: A written statement outlining the responsibilities for a particular job or group of jobs within the same organization. These responsibilities are related to the skills and background needed to complete the job successfully: education, similar work experience and skill level at certain tasks (knowledge of computer software, welding).

Job Evaluations: Once classified, jobs are systematically evaluated in a business setting to understand their value to the organization and its goals as well as in terms of setting compensation levels.

Job Rotation: Moving employees from one job to another within an organization in order to relieve sameness of the work-an opportunity to introduce new skills and work experiences. This may be part of a larger labor agreement or just customary and ordinary in a particular business or industry group.

Job Sharing: Two or more people who share a full-time job. Perhaps two part-time workers who make up one full-time position. It is one of many alternative employee work relationships that serve both employees and employers.

Jobber: A merchant that acts as a middleman and sells various products (often in bulk) and then resells them to different types of retailers. These individuals do not act for specific clients, but often specialize in selling specific types of products.

Joinder: Making common cause with another party with whom you share common questions of law or jurisdiction.

Joint and Several: When dealing with a financial issue this refers to a debt where each debtor is liable for the entire amount. The creditor then can collect the entire amount from any of the debtors or both of the debtors.

Joint Enterprise: Two or more individuals engage in an activity for their mutual benefit (although not necessarily always for profit), and this may entail a joint venture, partnership or another form of business type in which more than one of the individuals works, manages and invests for the agreed purpose of the enterprise. A court will often find liability for all parties making up a joint enterprise even though the negligent act or breach of contract resulted from just one person's actions.

Joint Insurance: Two or more parties, each with their own interests in the same property, insure the property under a single insurance policy with the same insurer.

Joint Liability: This is a situation where two or more people share the liability-responsibility for a claim, judgment or a debt. The person making the claim can bring into the suit all those deemed jointly liable

Joint Money Laundering Steering Group (JMLSG): A committee of British financial associations who have joined together to provide assistance to its members on the all-important issue of money laundering and how to interpret the United Kingdom's regulations.

Joint Tenancy: The joint ownership of real or personal property, thus guaranteeing the right of survivorship; does not require administration and frequently is not subject to death taxes.

Joint Venture: Where two or more individuals engage in an activity-limited and specific in its purpose-for profit (e.g., like flipping a home for profit by buying the home, renovating it and selling it). Although similar to a partnership in many ways, once the purpose of the joint venture ends and the bills are paid the joint venture itself terminates.

JORC: In Australia, the Joint Ore Reserves Committee which reports on exploration results, mineral reserves and ore reserves.

Ju'alal: Under Islamic law, some bank charges and commissions which are permitted under the law.

Judgment Creditor: This is the successful or winning party in a lawsuit in which a court has decided the defendant owes money. If the losing party files for bankruptcy then the judgment creditor assumes priority status over general, unsecured creditors that lack judgments, but it is up to the creditor to collect the money owed upon the initial judgment in his favor.

Judgment Debtor: This is the losing party, or defendant, in a lawsuit that has had a judgment against them and owes the amount of the judgment to the judgment creditor

Judicial Activism: Fostering of creative, legal precedence and rulings, often outside of the intent of the executive and legislative branches of government, which now take on legal standing.

Judicial Review: In the broadest interpretation, it is the way the courts will supervise (review) the government, industry regulators, local authorities and other public bodies to ensure that they act lawfully and fairly.

Judicial Sale: Often done to satisfy a judgment or court order, this is the sale of goods by an official appointed by the court.

Jurisdiction: The power to hear and adjudicate a matter before the court.

K

K: A symbol used often in legal practice and by law students, this shorthand mark signifies contract.

Kabushiki-kaivhi: Japanese for stock market.

Keeping in Touch Days: In the United Kingdom, an employee can work up to 10 days for their employer during maternity (adoption) leave without bringing an end to the maternity leave.

Key Man Life Insurance: A policy is taken out by the company on the life of a major executive or director (often partners is a small business) to which the company or partnership is the beneficiary in the event of death. The cash cushion allows the company to weather any business interruptions due to the executive's death.

Kickback: Where the seller of goods or services pays the buyer's agent of those goods or services a part of the purchase price with the intention of persuading the agent to enter into the transaction, as well as future transactions. Kickbacks are often illegal and fall within commercial bribery statutes.

Kidnap Insurance: As the concept implies, a corporation takes out an insurance policy in case a key executive is kidnapped for ransom. From time to time, organized crime is some countries have used kidnapping as a major source of revenue; wealthy individuals and foreign businessmen have been the targets because of their willingness to pay the ransom.

King's Bench: Can be the King's or Queen's Bench depending on who is the reigning monarch (*See* ***Queen's Bench***). In Great Britain this is the highest court of the land during the reign of a King.

Kiting Checks: The simple acting of writing checks against uncollected balances. Banks are not supposed to release funds until deposits are cleared. Kiting is illegal.

Know-how Licensing: Transferring technical information to another party allowing the other party to use this information for the production of goods or services; the transfer is based on the fact that the second party will pay a fee or license royalty for the use of the technology/information.

Know Your Customer (KYC): In an effort to prevent money laundering specifically, getting as much information about your customers-especially if sums involved are large-in an effort to prevent abuse of the banking system. The assumption is that the more you know about the customer, the better the chance of preventing fraud of any kind.

Known Loss: Both buyer and seller know that there is damage to goods that are about to be shipped or that are in route to the buyer. The known loss may change substantially the terms of sale, including refusal to accept at the time of receipt.

Kompetenz-Kompetenz: This is a well-established principle in international arbitration and it refers specifically to whether an arbitration tribunal has the jurisdiction to rule on a matter.

KYC: *See* ***know your customer***.

L

Labor Agreement: A contract between management and workers as to general terms of employment, including pay rates, benefits, working conditions, staffing levels and means of arbitrating future labor disputes. The agreement may be for just an individual work site or could be a master agreement covering all plants and offices owned and operated by the company.

Labor Intensive: Any type of business that requires extensive use of labor to produce goods or services. Many organizations of this kind cannot make use of technology or automation; labor intensive manufacturing has gravitated to regions and countries with low labor costs as a means to compensate for the inability to use assets to reduce costs. Customer service operations, unlike manufacturing, have moved to remote locations for the same reason: the need to find cheaper sources of labor.

LAFTA: Acronym for Latin American Free Trade Association, founded in 1960, and designed to be a common market (as in Europe) for Latin America. The goal is to foster mutual regional trade among members. It has never had the same success as the European Union.

Laissez-Faire: Essentially from the French for allow us to do (something), it has taken on the more specific connotation of nonintervention and noninterference of government in business. Often associated with Adam Smith in *The Wealth of Nations*, it is described as free enterprise with minimum governmental functions.

Land Registry: In England and Wales, the land registry is the government agency which records ownership to and interest in registered land. It also guarantees the title to all registered land.

Landed Value: A maritime insurance terms meaning the value of goods or products which have arrived at their intended destination; this is based on their wholesale not retail value.

Lapping: Embezzlement in which customer's cash payments are stolen and this activity is covered up by using other customer's cash payments to cover the first embezzlement and so forth.

Lapse: Typically relating to insurance, the termination of an unmatured policy by failing to pay the premium within the one month grace period. Despite a lapse, some policies may be reinstated by further payment.

Last in First Out: In the event of unemployment or job layoffs (redundancy), it is the method of selecting which employees will loose their employment based on the principle that those with the longest time of service are fired after those with little time of service, thus the last hired are the first to be fired.

Latent Defect: A flaw or imperfection that is hidden to the buyer through normal inspection, but which the seller knows about and which usually entitles the buyer to their money back; in the converse, to demand a replacement without the imperfection or defect under the auspices of implied warranty of merchantability. As-is bought material purchased with a latent defect can also be a reason to rescind the purchase if shown that the seller knew of the defect

Latin American Free Trade Association: *See* *LAFTA*.

Law Commission: In England and Wales, the Law Commission was established in 1965 to oversee existing laws and through its publications and other efforts, makes recommendations on how to simplify and modernize the law.

Law of Agency: All of the legal issues surrounding an individual or entity which functions as a representative (agent) of another individual or entity, acting on the first party's behalf, with full legal authority to carry out the agreed upon responsibilities.

Law of Demand: Simply, the amount of a certain product (or service) which consumers are willing to purchase. There is a predictable relationship between price and quantity demanded. If demand is high, the price will rise; if demand is low, the price must decrease, thus the law of demand.

Lawyer-Client Relationship: It is the role of the attorney to protect the interests of his client at all time, so that nothing said in a lawyer-client relationship can be used against the client. It is privileged.

Lay Days: The agreed upon or contracted number of days by which a ship is supposed to be loaded or unloaded.

Layers: In a complicated insurance deal, one that potentially could cost an insurer a great deal of money in the event of a loss, several companies will insure the project or asset whereby the risk is layered and each insurance company is responsible for a layer of the risk management.

Lead Bank: In a corporate workout or restructuring, it is not uncommon to have a number of lenders, particularly if the firm is a large one. Typically, the bank with the largest exposure and/or the most experience in restructuring deals similar to this one will become the lead bank. After notifying other creditors, they will take the lead in the steering committee throughout the process.

Lease: A contract granting or letting possession and control of buildings, land, machinery or offices for a specific period of time in consideration of periodic payments for its use-rent. Upon termination of the lease or failure to make payments or failure to fill other standards in a lease agreement the property's control reverts to the owner.

Lease Guarantee: A program of the Export-Import Bank of the United States that guarantees loans to foreign buyers of American-made goods (also includes services). The guarantee covers both principal and interest and is designed to help companies compete internationally.

Legacy: A gift of property or money made by the will of a testator. A legacy can constitute various forms and have a variety of conditions attached to it.

Legal Professional Privilege: A fundamental common law right that allows a litigant to withhold certain evidence during the course of a judicial hearing or other proceeding. There are two of these privileges: Legal advice privilege allows for confidential communication between lawyer and client in the pursuit of the client's goal in seeking legal advice and litigation privilege which also allows private communications between lawyers and their clients as it related to an actual case or pending litigation.

Legislative Intent: When a law is enacted, what is the real meaning or intent of the law by the lawmakers? Anyone seeking to interpret the law (a judge, for example), but must go back and examine the legislative intent (history).

Less Developed Countries: Sometimes call third world countries, those countries whose economic development lags substantially behind the so-called first world countries (Japan, Germany, United Kingdom, etc). The economies are characterized by high dependence on extraction, commodities, fuels, raw materials and basic agriculture.

Letter of Credit: Generally a means to advance domestic and foreign trade, it substitutes the bank's credit for the individual or corporation. A commercial letter of credit will assure a seller that he will be paid by submitting an invoice for payment directly to the bank.

Letter of Intent: Sometimes used in mergers when two company plan to join into one, it is a statement that the parties are willing and able to do so. Otherwise it can be a written statement to a third party indicating something that will be done in the near future, e.g. pay off our business loan.

Leverage: One uses borrowed money to buy real property, or possibly business assets. Often the borrowed money equals a high percentage of the value of the purchased property. Leverage implies high risk as the income from the investment may not be sufficient to cover the costs of borrowing.

Leveraged Buyout: A smaller business, for example, purchases a larger business, for example, with funds generated by borrowing on the assets of the company being bought and using them as security.

Levies: Commonly called tariffs or import duties imposed on goods entering a foreign country.

Liability: In financial terminology, this is the debt of an individual or entity. In legal terminology, this refers to an individual's or entity's legal responsibility for its acts or omissions.

Liability Insurance: Protection to policyholders from financial loss due to liability from injuries to other persons or loss from damage to their property.

Liable: Legally responsible or obligated. For example, an individual who caused damages in an accident can be found liable for those damages, or a co-signor on a loan can be found liable to repay that debt.

Libel: An untrue characterization of another individual or corporation whose intent is to be malicious, thus harming the good name of that individual. Libel can be in writing, printed in a newspaper or even pictures. Proof of libel can result in huge monetary rewards.

LIBOR: Acronym for the London Interbank Offer Rate, a benchmark for financial dealings, more particularly the rate at which banks lend money to other banks. LIBOR is often used as the base to determine rates for mortgages, commercial lending and credit cards, among other transactions.

Licensing: The use of another's trademark, patent, copyrighted material, technology or software, for example, by a second part for a fee or royalty. The license can be limited or open ended and can have options for future versions of the item licensed.

Lien: A claim by a creditor against property or money that is the result of nonpayment of a debt, or for money owed based on services rendered by another.

Life Interest Trust: Generally a kind of private trust from which a life tenant is entitled to receive a fixed income for life or for a fixed period of time. Upon death, the life interest trust may terminate or pass on to another individual.

Limit Pricing: Attempts by a small group of companies to prevent others from entering their market by making prices extremely low; typically, there are few sellers so the intent is to control the market. Generally considered an illegal practice by restraining trade and commerce.

Limited Liability: Dealing with claims against a business, this is the maximum amount a business owner or investor stands to lose if the business is subject to any debts or claims made against the business. While a general partner may be, and usually is, responsible for all the debts of a partnership, a limited partner will only be responsible for his or her investment.

Limited Liability Company (LLC): This type of business ownership provides its owners with only limited personal liability, while still offering its owners a voice in the way the business will be taxed.

Limited Liability Partnership (LLP): This is a type of partnership which provides each individual partner with protection from personal liability with regards to negligent acts of other partners or of an employee not under his or her control

Limited Recourse Loan: This is a common kind of financing for large projects, say building a refinery or a new road. The bank or lender is entitled to interest or principal only on receipt of specific income streams or the availability of capital assets to satisfy those payments. Should the borrower default, the lender can recover only a limited amount of any shortfall from the originator of the loan. Thus, its recourse is said to be limited.

Line Extension: A well-known consumer brand is used on new products, not necessarily related to the original line. Crayola, for example, has extended its line of packaged crayons by branding a whole series of toys and art supplies for children-thus a line extension. This can also be a licensing agreement with another entity-a fast food provider is granted a license for a specific version of an existing product for use in its promotions and advertising.

Line of Credit: The amount of money an individual or company may borrow from a bank at any give time. It is the total amount of credit available to the borrower. Lines of credit will increase (or decrease) depending on the financial and business conditions of the borrower.

Liquid assets: These are assets of a business that can be sold/converted into money (e.g., shares).

Liquidate: To sell off the assets of a company for its money value, and then use the money to pay off any outstanding bills and then divide the left over money amongst shareholders, investors and/or partners.

Liquidated Damages: Often specified in a contract, this is a predetermined amount that a defaulting party will have to pay if he breaches a contract.

Liquidated Value: The price a company can and is willing to accept when it is forced to sell assets, either to satisfy creditors or because of bankruptcy.

Liquidity: How easily a company can convert it assets to cash to pay debts; it is assumed that liquid assets are easily able to be sold and thus not suffer any loss in value while illiquid assets are more difficult to sell (or take longer) and may suffer loss of value in the process. Selling blue chip stocks (liquid) is easier and faster than selling real estate (illiquid).

List(s): In the United Kingdom, it is a form used in civil proceedings which states which relevant documents a party has and will allow the opponent to inspect; which documents a party has but will not allow inspection by the opponent and finally documents which a party had but no longer has access to them. Some explanation as to the process of discovery (searching for) these documents is also included.

Listed Building: In the United Kingdom, these are buildings of specific architectural or historical interest, the goal of which is to protect such buildings from being torn down or altered inappropriately.

Listed Building Consent: The local planning authority has the ability to consent to demolition of a listed building or any part of it, or altering the interior or the exterior of the building that would adversely affect its character. Really important buildings are not under control of the local planning authority but the English Heritage.

LLC: *See* ***limited liability corporation***.

Lloyds Registry: A list or ranking of ships and vessels by Lloyds, categorized by types. The typing is important as it directly affects shipping rates, insurance, the quality of the personnel and so forth.

Lloyds: An association of English insurance underwriters, perhaps the oldest in the world. Policies are not written by the association, but by its individual members. Members must have certain minimums in assets and cash reserves but also are expected to assume unlimited personal liability in the event of a major loss.

LLP: *See* ***limited liability partnership***.

Loan Syndication: Either because the financial package was very large or no bank wanted to assume the risk on its own, a group of banks join together to form a lending syndication for a high-risk project. They share gains and losses in proportion to their participation.

Lobbyist: An individual or company hired by companies, private organizations or just about anyone who wants to influence the political process. The lobbyist's job is to engage government officials and try to influence their thinking and voting on specific issues important to the client.

Lock in Agreement: An agreement to lock disputing parties in until they reach some kind of compromise or agreement.

Lock Out: In industrial labor actions, employers can close their place of business (lock out employees) as pressure to settle a labor action. Further, they may open their place of business with temporary workers (often called scabs) during a strike; the added pressure tends to inflame the situation, not bring the parties together.

Locked In: Guarantee of a fixed rate for the term of a loan, for example, no matter what happens to interest rates. If they go up, the borrower benefits; if they go down, the borrower generally does not benefit and may seek another loan to replace this one to take advantage of lower interest charges.

Lombard Loans: In England and the E.U., loans secured by bonds and shares. It gets its name from Lombard Street, the Wall Street of London.

London Approach: The Bank of England in the 1970s developed a series of guidelines and principles which govern and direct a company's bankers and other creditors on how to respond to the news that a company is having a liquidity problem.

London Fix: Twice a day, a group of bankers determine the price of gold by matching buy and sell orders.

***London Gazette*:** This is the official newspaper of the British Royal Crown. It contains a wide range of public and governmental notices, even some that are statutory in nature and used in legal proceedings.

London Interbank Offered Rate: *See LIBOR*.

Long-Arm Statute: A United States law that provides local courts with the ability to expand their jurisdiction to an out-of-state business or individual that caused damage locally; allowing the court to pull them back under the states' laws. The test used by the courts is whether the business or individual had sufficiently substantial contact within the state.

Long-term Incentive Plan: Companies will arrange to reward senior managers and directors with shares in the company at a favorable price, partly for past performance but also as an incentive to remain with the company. Often specific benchmarks are included before compensation (all or some) is granted.

Loro Accounts: Current accounts of banks with foreign banks of a foreign currency held on behalf of a customer.

Loss of Bargain: When a party to a contract breaches that contract or a party intentionally interferes with a business, or a party is responsible for some other wrong doing, and this action results in an inability to complete a deal or sale.

Loss: In financial terms, when profits are less than expenses.

M

MAC: *See material adverse change.*

Mailbox Rule: In contract law, this is when a written contract is offered or accepted via the mail service (making the offer valid), and it has correct postage and is put in the mail within the allotted time frame, the offer must be accepted-barring a situation where it is agreed by the parties that acceptance requires personal delivery.

Major Multinationals: The world's giant petroleum companies: Chevron, Royal Dutch, Exxon-Mobil, BP-Amoco and Texaco.

Make: When dealing with financial issues, this refers to the signing of a check, promissory note or other note/document that guarantees, orders or promises payment of money.

Maker: This refers to the individual that signs a promissory note, check or other type of note and is responsible for payment on the note. This designation may also refer to an individual who endorses a promissory note or check over to another individual before it is delivered. In this situation the endorser is duty-bound to pay on the document until it is delivered.

Malingerer: Faking illness at the work place, perhaps to avoid certain unpleasant tasks or duties.

Management Agreement: Allocation of administrative duties and departments among the senior managers of a company; established of managerial accountability for the various operations of an enterprise. This allocation may be part of both an employment contract as well as a formal job description, both of which can be legally binding.

Management Audit: Formal evaluation of management performance in terms of prescribed goals and objectives. This review may be part of an employment contract and as such defines the process as well as what, if any, benefit or further compensation may be due. The audit tends to be extensive and in-depth, perhaps setting out new goals and objectives before the next audit.

Management Buy In (MBI): Acquisition of a company, similar to a management buyout, but in this case a management team from outside the company leads the acquisition.

Management Buyout: Attempt by a company's management team (senior managers, typically) to acquire the company for which they work. Often, the financing for these kinds of deals comes from venture capital, bank debt financing or generally leveraging company assets to support the buyout plan.

Management by Objectives: *See MBO.*

Management Contracts: An agreement made with a foreign-owned firm to make seasoned managers available to that firm in order to improve operations.

Management Fee: Among others, a fee paid to a real estate management company for control and operation of a condominium, office complex or a shopping center. A management fee can be paid to almost any operation where ownership is absent and not active in the company.

Management Letter: An auditor's formal correspondence to an officer of a company making suggestions on improving procedures, operations and controls concerning accounting, finance, taxes and other management issues.

Management's Discussion and Analysis of Financial Condition and Results of Operations (MDS&A): These are disclosure requirements under U.S. securities laws. Companies registered with the Securities and Exchange Commission (SEC) must report and provide financial data quarterly and annually under very specific conditions and formats (10K, for example).

Mandate: A potential borrower gives in writing the authority to a lender to arrange financing or a loan, typically this is accompanied by a corporate resolution signed by the directors.

Manifest: When dealing with shipping, this refers to a written list of goods in shipment. It is part of the shipping contract as it specifies the goods to be delivered.

Manufacturer's Outfit Insurance Liability: Essential insurance purchased by a company to protect itself from liability from goods or products it manufacturers.

Marine Bill of Landing: Basically a contract for transportation of goods from one point to another between the shipper and the marine carrier. It is also a receipt for freight prepared by the shipper for goods going by sea.

Maritime Law: These are laws- together with international treaties and agreements-that oversee activities at sea or other navigable waters. This is also referred to as the law of admiralty and/or admiralty law.

Mark Signature: When an individual is unable to write his own name, he will affix his mark (an X or other identifying mark) to a contract, check or other legally binding document. The name of the signer is then printed next to the mark and witnessed. This constitutes a valid signature.

Mark to Market: This is an important element in accounting, and when abused, as in the infamous Enron case, can overstate earnings and profits. The company's balance sheet must show loans and debts at their fair market value, which may be higher or lower that the cost of acquiring these items. This accounting method is often restricted to specific kinds of businesses, such as banks or loan companies.

Market Abuse: Almost all major economies with sophisticated financial and capital markets place limitations on specific behavior on the part of individuals and companies. Some examples are: insider trading, not providing full disclosure or improper disclosure, misuse of information, distortion or insider information-just about any behavior that is intended to defraud or limit the fairness of the marketplace.

Market Capitalization: How a company which is listed on a public exchange would be valued. Typically, but simplistically, it is the number of shares issued times the then current price at which the shares are traded. Because both variables are ever-changing, the market capitalization of a public company can change rapidly and wildly at times.

Market Disruption: Foreign goods are dumped in the domestic market; the net effect is that prices for similar goods fall, often drastically. Generally, dumping of any kind is illegal.

Market Value: This is the price that property or another item would bring if offered in the open market for sale (does not include an auction or foreclosure sale).

Marks of Origin: All countries require that goods coming into the country be marked with the country of origin. Often this has to be on the labeling or packaging of the product as well.

Master: A judge in the Royal Courts of Justice in the United Kingdom who has the authority to hear applications for summary judgments and to assess damages.

Master and Servant: Dealing with the relationship between an employer and employee, this is the body of law that concerns this relationship. *See* ***respondent superior*** for further information regarding this relationship.

Master Development Agreement: A franchise agreement which allows an franchisee the right to operate within a specific area, but does not allow the franchisee to sub-franchise to other third parties.

Master Franchise Agreement: A company can allow what is called a master franchise agreement whereby an individual is allowed to grant franchises to third parties within a specified territory.

Material Adverse Change (MAC) Clause: A fairly standard agreement which allows the buyer the right to walk away from a potential corporate acquisition before the closing time in the event that events detrimental to the about-to-be-acquired company are exposed. A lawsuit, a loss of an important customer or incorrect financial information may be sufficient justification and thus defined as material adverse changes.

Materiality: Information that would be significant or important to an informed investor or lender when making a decision to invest or lend to a company or an individual. Loss of a major customer or non-conforming accounting would be considered materiality.

Maternity Allowance: A benefit period of either 26 weeks or 39 weeks, depending upon circumstances, whereby women employees are paid for their time off for child birth in the United Kingdom.

Maturity: This represents the date in which payment of the principal amount is due on a bill of exchange or promissory note. Often the note itself states that a failure to make installment payments or pay interest accelerates the due date of the note and effectively moves up the maturity date of the note.

MBI: *See* ***management buy in***

MBO: Acronym for management by objectives, or a management system whereby managers and their teams establish standards for performance and goals to be met over a specific period of time, e.g. quarterly or annually. MBOs may be part of an employment agreement or performance contract.

MDA: Acronym for multiple discriminant analysis, or a credit guide scoring system which determines whether a borrower is creditworthy or not. It is a statistically-based ranking system, scoring points for certain kinds of behavior and data in a customer's credit record.

MDS&A: *See* ***management discussion and analysis of financial condition and results of operations***.

Mechanic's Lien: A claim in favor of payment for work done to a building or other property. The landlord has not paid the roofer, and so he places a mechanic's lien against not only the building but the property as well until payment is made. The property may not be sold until the lien is removed. It is a preferred claim and must be paid before any other claims, except taxes.

Mediation: A situation where parties to a dispute attempt to utilize the services of a third party, outside the courts, to aid in settling the dispute. While mediation differs from arbitration, because the arbitrator acts more like a judge, the mediator actively participates in the discussion to help solve disputes. Mediation does not always result in a settlement. Mediation or arbitration are often included as boilerplate clauses in a contract, especially those which involve small matters or sums of money.

Meeting of the Minds: When both parties to an agreement agree on the terms of a contract and each party understands the terms of the agreement.

Memorandum of Association: A corporate document filed with the Companies House in the United Kingdom which states the official name, address, nature of its business, capital and its liabilities. This information is then in the public domain and may be read and copied by anyone.

Merchantable: Where a product is fit for sale and is without damages or flawed in some capacity so as to render it usable for the purpose it was designed. It is an implied guarantee of quality, meeting some basic standard.

Merger: When dealing with corporations, this is two or more corporate entities combine to form one corporation with the assets of the fusing corporation to be transferred to the other, now parent corporation. Although one company in effect absorbs another company, shareholders from the absorbed company receive shares of the new company.

Mezzanine Debt: Often a second level of debt, below senior debt (a bank loan secured by assets) but higher than trade credits and trade debts. The debt is secured and may be guaranteed by the principals of the firm. Often this kind of debt can be converted into common shares of the company.

Minimum Wage: First referred to as a living wage by Pope Leo XIII, it is now the statutory mandated basic wage which can be offered an employee per hour worked. Almost all countries with sophisticated economies have minimum wage laws. They are, from time to time, adjusted for inflation.

Ministry of International Trade and Industry (MITI): Government agency in Japan charged with managing trade policy and overseeing export industries.

Minutes: This is a written record, often of meetings with shareholders and/or boards of directors, detailing the goings-on within the meetings, and is often taken by the secretary of the corporation.

Misappropriation: An illegal act, where the perpetrator intentionally uses the funds and/or property of another for his or her own use, and for an unauthorized purpose, e.g., a public official or fiduciary.

Misfeasance: Where an unfortunate result within in a business occurs due to errors, mistakes or carelessness, but which have not been committed with the intent to violate the law or with an evil intent (e.g., an actual mistake by a corporate counsel).

Misrepresentation: Essentially an untrue statement made by one party to another which causes the second party to enter into an agreement and to suffer some kind of loss as a result of the misrepresentation. There are three kinds of misrepresentation: fraudulent, where a false statement has been made knowingly; negligent, where a statement is made carelessly without checking the facts; and innocent, whereby no attempt to defraud or otherwise cause harm was intended.

MITI: *See* ***Ministry of International Trade and Industry***.

Mitigation: There is a duty under a contract to lessen any possible negative outcomes. So, a claimant cannot recover damages for part of a loss which he could have avoided by taking reasonable steps. The acid test is what are reasonable steps.

Mixer Cap: As part of the Finance Act 2000 in the United Kingdom, the use of offshore mixer companies to increase foreign tax credits allowed against U.K. taxes is negated.

Model Law: This is an attempt to get countries to adopt similar or the same laws in efforts to coordinate arbitration laws and proceedings. While many countries have adopted the model law entirely or in part, the United Kingdom does not accept the whole law.

Modified Dismissal Procedures: In the labor environment in the United Kingdom, an employer may dismiss an employee without notice under circumstances of gross misconduct. It can only be used if it is reasonable for the employer to dismiss the employee before making any inquiries as to the employee's behavior or conduct-in other words, the situation is extreme and demands immediate action.

Money Broker: An intermediary between a borrower and a lender.

Money Claim: The claim is designed to recover money, as opposed to other remedies available to the claimant: return of property, an injunction or a cease and desist order.

Moneyed Corporation: Typically, any company or corporation formed under the banking or insurance laws and subject to the same.

Monoline Insurer: A specialized insurance business whose only business is writing financial guarantee insurance. This kind of insurance may be required as part of a loan or other commercial contract or agreement.

Monopoly: A situation where one company is the sole provider to an industry, thereby controlling that industry and controlling a great deal of the production or sale of products. Essentially these companies control the market with regards to said products, including prices and distribution. Certain federal statutes and antitrust laws are in place to keep tabs on, and if appropriate, prohibit monopolies and restraint of trade.

Monopsony: A market where there is only one buyer for a product. A local, isolated area has only one buyer of locally produced produce.

Moral Right: In the matter of intellectual property rights, an individual is allowed to be acknowledged as the author of a work and also has the right to protect the work from any derogatory treatment.

Moral Risk: Generally referrers to the honesty or integrity of a borrower seeking a loan. Can a person be trusted to repay the loan, no matter how great the resources with which to repay the loan. Many consider moral risk the most important element in lending.

Moratorium: Where repayment of a loan is extended or suspended (often only for a brief period). An example would be where the right to debt collection is halted by bankruptcy.

Mortgage: A temporary pledge of property to a lender as security for repayment of a loan. A house is mortgaged until the final payment is made to the bank, where upon a clear title is issued to the buyer.

Muniment of Title: A document by which certain rights are fortified or maintained. A bill of lading, besides being a receipt of goods, is a muniment of title.

Mudarabah: Under Islamic law, the investor provides capital to the entrepreneur; profits are shared on agreed upon basis, while losses are borne by the investor alone.

Mudarib: The investor in an Islamic Mudarabah.

Murabaha (Cost-plus Financing): A financial institution buys an asset from a supplier and then sells it to a customer at a fixed price that is higher than the purchase price. The agreement is not a violation of sharia in Islamic law because the financial institution takes title to the assets and takes on the risks and therefore is entitled to a profit.

Musharaka (Equity and Venture Capital Financing): A joint venture under Islamic law whereby the bank or financial institution and the investor provide financing for a specific project in agreed proportions. The parties share equally in the profit and loss. This structure is possible under sharia since the partnership is based on the principles of share in and benefiting from risk.

Mutual Recognition: Documents prepared under the laws of one jurisdiction are recognized as compliant with the laws of another jurisdiction.

Mutuality of Obligations: The relationship of an employee and an employer is based on the existence of a mutually binding legal obligation, e.g. a contract for an employer to pay and for an employee to work.

N

NAFTA: *See North American Free Trade Agreement.*

Name: An underwriting member of Lloyds. Members are expected to have met strict financial standards before being accepted and join with other members to underwrite business. They personally are responsible for any losses, but also gain personally in any profits made by the various syndicates.

NASD: *See below, National Association of Securities Dealers.*

National Association of Securities Dealers (NASD): It is the largest self-regulatory securities organization in the United States. Because it is supervised by the Securities and Exchange Commission (SEC), almost all institutions, trading houses and banks who deal with securities in the over-the-counter market are members. Its basic role is to regulate and control the industry, including investigating any instances of fraud or wrongdoing.

National Bank: A bank authorized or chartered by the federal or national government. It typically manages interest rates and the liquidity of funds in the banking system.

National Debt: The total of all bonds, notes, bills, certificates of indebtedness and any other obligations of the national or federal government of a country. National debt is often described or expressed as a percentage of gross national product (GNP).

National Insurance Contributions (NICs): In the United Kingdom, this is the total amount payable by employers, employees and the self-employed to HM Revenue & Customs. It is a percentage of earnings, with the lowest earners paying little or nothing and with a cap on earnings beyond a certain level.

Nationalization: Generally a forced takeover of private property, industry, natural resources or other assets by a foreign government, with or without compensation. While new local ownership may be the majority stake holder, at times the original company is left with some portion of the company or assets.

National Minimum Wage: In the United Kingdom, a minimum hourly rate of pay is set by the government. There are actually three rates: adult workers over age 22, a training rate for workers aged 18 to 21 and a third rate for workers 16 and 17 years of age.

National Monopoly: A monopoly is allowed because it is more efficient than to have more than one supplier, e.g. a gas or electric company. It is not cost efficient for there to be more than one supplier, although with many countries experimenting with deregulation, natural monopolies are less frequent than in the past.

Natural Person: Distinguished from a corporation, which is usually treated as a fictitious person, this is a real human being.

Near Money: Liquid assets that are like money, meaning that they can be converted to cash quickly: stocks, bonds and money market funds.

Negative Assurance: Literally telling a legal or accounting client that nothing unusual came to his attention, therefore everything is fine. Such correspondence is intended to assuage the concerns or fears of the client about unforeseen circumstances. Basically, no news is good news.

Negative Pledge: It is a covenant in a loan agreement that prevents a debtor from using certain assets or security as a pledge for other debt without prior written consent of the initial lender. The goal on the part of the first lender is to ensure that it has preferred claim if the loan defaults.

Negligence: A failure to exercise care considered appropriate under the circumstances, resulting in unintentional loss or injury to a third party. A landlord fails to fix a broken step; a company's product causes injury during ordinary use.

Negligent Misstatement: Often confused with negligent misrepresentations, negligent misstatement may be a basis for action even though the parties are not in any way contractually linked. A statement is made carelessly and it causes harm to a third party-who is indirectly or directly linked-even though not contractually so.

Negotiable Instrument: A signed, written promise to transfer a specified sum of money on demand to the name on the instrument, the bearer. Negotiable instruments can be endorsed and transferred to a third party.

Negotiated Trade: Rather than influenced by the free market, a government manages the trading process.

Negotiation: When dealing with finance, this term refers to the transfer of a negotiable instrument from one to another for money, goods, services or some other benefit.

Net: The amount left over-of money or value-after taxes, charges, losses, etc., have been removed, paid or subtracted.

Network: Other business professionals in your acquaintance; often useful in getting information or when seeking employment.

NICs: *See* ***national insurance contributions***.

Ninow Account: A deposit or account with an intermediary on which no interest or dividend is paid; a holding account for future payments to a third party.

Nominal: Equal to purchasing power, this is the net earned wages without considering the effects of inflation.

Noncompetition Agreement: Used in an employment contract and contracts for the sale of a business, this is a provision put into the agreement by both parties which provides that one person (usually the person being employed or the person selling the business) will not compete with the other party for a specified period of time and/or within a certain, specified, geographical location. Different states and countries have various restrictions on these types of agreements.

Noncontestability Clause: In insurance, a standard clause in a policy which prevents the insurer from contesting the validity of the policy on the basis of fraud or mistake; the policy must be in effect for several years before this is valid. The assumption is that the company would have had sufficient time to find and correct the mistakes or errors.

Nondischaregable Debts: These are debts that will not be extinguished by filing for bankruptcy, and they include alimony, most student loans, child support, income tax, as well as personal injury debts.

Nondisclosure Agreement: A contract which binds one party to a promise not to disclose certain information that would be characterized as a trade secret to others, unless allowed to do so. This agreement may be deemed implied depending on the nature of the work being done.

Non-dumping Certificate: The exporter certifies that the goods coming into the country are being sold at a price equal to or similar to the same kind of products made in the importing country.

Nonfeasance: Where an employee (an agent of an employer) fails to perform a duty he or she agreed to do for his or her employer (principal).

Non-profit Corporation: A corporation operating for educational, charitable, social, religious, civic or humanitarian purposes and which is approved as such under state laws and by the state's Secretary of State and its taxing authority. Although this type of corporation has a board of directors and officers, it does not have shareholders, and while it can make a profit, any proceeds from the profit must go to, and benefit the corporation.

Non-recourse Loan: A loan secured by property alone, typically used in commercial or income property lending. The borrowing history and the character of the borrower are particularly important for this kind of lending.

No-par Stock: These are corporate shares which are issued, but which do not have a price-per-share stated within a stock certificate. The value of these shares is reflected at the current stock market price.

North American Free Trade Agreement (NAFTA): A trade agreement that over a 10 year period would eliminate trade restrictions between and among Canada, Mexico and the United States. In effect, it is a free trade zone.

Nostro Accounts: A bank or financial institution in one country which has balances deposited in corresponding banks in another country.

Note: Simply is a written promise to pay another person a certain amount by a specified date-a promissory note.

Notice: A formal notification under contract law that the contract is to end at a certain point. A well-written contract will specify the amount of notice time required, e.g. 90 days.

Notice of Appeal: In the context of British employment law, this document is used to lodge an appeal against an employment tribunal concerning a decision by that tribunal.

Notice on Agreements of Minor Importance: Frequently called the de minimis notice, this is a notice published by the E.C. whether an agreement between parties with only small market share is likely to be an infringement on free trade.

Notice of Default: A formal, written notice to a debtor that a loan is in default. Often this is a legal requirement before the lender can take action against the debtor; presumably the debtor has an opportunity to make good on the loan.

Novation: This occurs when parties to an older contract agree to substitute it for a new contract, thus canceling the old contract.

Nugatory: Having no force or effect. For example, a law found to be unconstitutional by the U.S. Supreme Court is a nugatory law.

Nuisance: A public nuisance is an act that endangers life, health, property, morals and the general comfort of the community while a private nuisance is an action done on private property, which a person is normally entitled to do, but which goes beyond private property and affects the larger public in general.

NV: An indication of a public company in the Netherlands. It is typically capitalized through the sales of stock or shares and is a limited liability company.

O

Obiter: Known as *obiter dictum* or a saying in passing. An expression or opinion by a judge, but one that is not essential and is not binding.

Objectivity: That which is said to be free of bias, unusual influence, prejudice or personal feelings. Objectivity is the cornerstone of contracts, the law and even arbitration; it assumes that all parties hearing or otherwise administering a case or action will act without predetermined opinions as to the individual parties to the case. An effort to decide on a matter based on its application to the law.

Obligation: A duty, legal in nature, to do something or make payment to another, including all classes of indebtedness; the debtor is bound to pay and the creditor has the legal right to compel payment.

Obligee: This is the individual or business owed an obligation by another, e.g., owed payment on a negotiable instrument.

Obligor: This is an individual that owes an individual or entity an obligation, e.g., the person that must pay on a negotiable instrument.

Occam's Razor: A general theory which emphasizes simplicity. First promulgated by William of Occam, the simplest workable theories are also the most useful and naturally the best.

Occupational Hazard: In certain types of employment or places of work, there is an inherent danger or risk associated with the type of work involved. Examples of these types of occupations include commercial fishing, skyscraper window washing, lumbering, etc.

Occupational Safety and Health Act (OSHA): This is the federal law that regulates and establishes safety standards in places of work in the United States.

Occurrence Policy: A liability insurance policy that covers claims that take place during the policy period (time of coverage) regardless of when the claim is filed. A remote property is damaged and the owner does not know about the incident until long after his policy has lapsed. He still has the right to make a claim as the damage was done during the life of the policy.

OECD: Acronym for The Organization For Economic Cooperation and Development, founded in 1948 to first help administer the Marshal Plan after World War II. While the mandate is very broad, it covers social and economic development of member nations. In recent years it has worked on the problem of spam on the Internet, as well as problems of corruption and bribery in government and in business.

Off-balance Sheet: Any asset, liability or financial commitment, for example a lease, which is not reflected on the company's balance sheet. (In many cases, though, this kind of activity will be reflected in the notes accompanying financial statements.) There is a legal, fiduciary responsibility to report this kind of activity in some way or other.

Offer: Where a proposition is made by one party to another regarding a specific proposal in order to enter into an agreement with that other party. This is one of the essential elements for entering into a contract (the others being acceptance and consideration). Once all three elements are satisfied an enforceable contract is usually created.

Offeror: In the United Kingdom according to the City Code on Takeovers and Mergers (the Code), any company or individual who is making or intends to make an offer for another company.

Officers: The directors of a stock corporation may chose from among themselves or outsiders as president, vice president, secretary and treasurer, among others, to direct, manage and otherwise operate the corporation on behalf of the shareholders.

Official: With regards to businesses, this individual is an officer of a corporation or business, and is hired by a board of directors, owner of a business or manager of an LLC, with the task of managing the day-to-day operations of the company.

Official Listing Notice: A formal notice from a stock exchange that the shares of the corporation have been accepted for listing on that exchange.

Official Receiver: An officer of the court or other individual appointed by the court who deals with bankruptcies and liquidations; basically his role is to manage and ensure the integrity of the assets involved in a liquidation and see the bankruptcy through the winding up stage.

Offset: The right of a bank or other lender to seize deposits to cover a loan in default.

Offshore Corporation: This is a corporation not charted under the laws of the host country, but rather under the laws of another country. Corporations are often charted under these countries (like those in the Caribbean) because they offer less stringent corporate regulations and offer lower, more advantageous, tax rates.

Offshore Finance Subsidiary: A subsidiary of a company is created and located outside of the host country for the purpose of facilitating banking, financial transactions and tax matters in that foreign country.

Okum's Law: A statistical relationship between unemployment and economic growth says that if economic growth is 3.5 percent to 4 percent, unemployment levels will remain the same as this equals the approximate number of people entering the job market. Only growth over 4 percent will decrease the unemployment rate.

Old Lady of Threadneedle Street: A nickname for the Bank of England, whose main entrance is on Threadneedle Street.

Oligopoly: There are only a few sellers for a product or a service, as a result they have substantial ability to control prices and quantities produced.

On Demand: A requirement of a promissory note, in which the amount due must be paid when the individual owed the funds demands payment (as opposed to installment payments or on a specified date). These are referred to as demand notes.

On or Before: Often found within the language of a contract or promissory note, this phrase requires payment or performance by a particular date or earlier.

OPEC: Acronym for the Organization of Petroleum Exporting Countries, founded in 1965 and headquartered in Vienna, it is an international oil cartel designed specifically to control the production and pricing of oil. As a group, it accounts for about 2/3rds of the world known supplies of oil. It is perhaps the most influential organization worldwide in that the decisions by the cartel affect directly every economy in the world.

Open Distribution: No limits on the number of dealers who may sell a particular product line in a geographical area. The distribution is unrestricted.

Open Insurance Policy: A policy covering all of a company's exports, not just one particular shipment or shipments made at a specific time.

Open Market Value: When property is offered for sale, open market value is the best price that might reasonably be expected for the property from a third party who has no direct ties to or interest in the selling property. Other, similar properties in the area would be used by the appraiser to determine the open market value.

Open Offer: New shares are offered to existing shareholders at a discount; specific amounts are allocated and if one shareholder declines or takes less than the offered allotment, other shareholders have the right to take up any excess shares in the open offer.

Open Shop: An employer's location that allows for both unionized and non-unionized employees.

Operating Company: As opposed to a holding company, an organization which operates or performs actual manufacturing or merchandizing-that actively conducts business.

Operating Lease: Often used to acquire equipment for a short period of time, during the busy season for example; the lessee acquires the equipment for a small portion of its useful economic life, without an expectation to buy the equipment at the end of the lease.

Opinion: An auditor's views as to the condition of the company and its financial statements; an opinion can be unqualified, adverse or a disclaimer, whereby the auditor is unable to offer an opinion as to the state of the business.

Opinion Letter: Any legal opinion from a lawyer which will be relied on by a third party considering some kind of business transaction or legal action. The caveat is, of course, that it is only an opinion and does not provide assurance as to accuracy.

Opportunity Cost: The cost of failing to act-making an investment or purchasing an asset-which presumably resulted in an opportunity that could have been productive or profitable.

Option: In contractual dealings, this is a right to require another to perform or to purchase property, and this is paid for as part of the contract. An option does require that it be exercised in order for the performance of the other party, or the purchase of the property, to be required. Often, to exercise the option, payment of the contract price, as well as notice, must be given.

Oral Contract: An agreement made between parties with spoken words, and without details being put in a writing (or there could possibly be a partial writing). Although an oral contract has the same validity as a written contract, if a dispute arises it can be much more difficult to prove the terms of the agreement.

Order: An instruction by a court or other legal tribunal in the favor of one party or the other in litigation.

Ordinary Resolution: A simple resolution that is passed by the majority of shareholders at the company general meeting. Notice to shareholders is required by the company when a shareholder's general meeting is scheduled. The goal is not to limit attendance unnecessarily.

Organization for Economic Co-operation and Development: *See OECD*

Organization of Petroleum Exporting Countries: *See OPEC*.

Origination Fee: A bank fee charged to a borrower for the costs associated with a loan; generally it covers commissions and other costs. Often part of a mortgage, for example.

OSHA: *See* ***Occupational Safety and Health Act***.

Ostensible Agent: An individual that has been given, or appears to have been given, the appearance of an employee or agent that is acting on behalf of another (principal), leaving those dealing with this individual with the belief that this person is a representative of his principal. Actions taken by such an individual can leave a company liable for damages or contractual commitments.

Outgoings: The costs and expenses incurred by the owner of a piece of property in connection with that ownership: insurance, repairs, maintenance, management and taxes, for example.

Out-of-Pocket Expenses: These are expenses incurred and paid directly by employees, trustees, contractors, etc., and which are to cover expenses not laid out within an agreement.

Output Contract: A written document in which a producer of products agrees to sell all of its production to a buyer, who in turn, through an agreement, agrees to purchase the entire output.

Outsourcing: Transferring business functions and personnel which were once done internally to an outside vendor or provider. The overall goal is to provide better service/quality or to save money.

Over-commitment: Contracting or making financial decisions that can not be paid for or are beyond the means of the corporation (or individual)-in excess of one's capital or credit.

Over Plus: A balance over all expenses or a surplus.

Overturn: Turnover or sales for a period.

Owe: Where a legal duty exist in which a debtor, or borrower, is required to pay back a certain sum to another.

P

Package: Before a contract is binding, all the several items that make up the agreement which must be accepted for the contract to be binding.

Panel on Takeovers and Mergers: This is a regulatory body in the United Kingdom whose role is to issue and enforce the City Code on Takeovers and Mergers and oversee its daily application. The goal is to make sure that both the spirit as well as the letter of the code are applied. Members are officers and managers of financial institutions and professional societies.

Panic: A sudden and unreasonable collapse in confidence in the banking system. One sign of a financial panic is a lack of cash liquidity in the business environment. Oddly a panic is preceded by a period of strong, even feverish, industrial expansion. While the actual panic may last just a few days, its after effects usually result in recession and unemployment.

Par: The represented (printed on a certificate) face value of a stock or bond, which indicates the amount originally paid for the stock or bond to the issuing corporation. No-par stock, however, is often representative of most common stocks, and as such, they lack a stated price per share, with the value instead reflected by the current market rate for the stock. If a stock is a preferred stock, it states a par value, or fixed rate, upon which dividends are calculated.

Paradox of Thrift: A seeming contradiction, the theory states that more savings may not always be good for the economy. While the general principle is that money saved is then borrowed and invested to grow the economy, too much savings crimps consumer consumption and the economy slows, with incomes reduced.

Parent Company: A company that owns (possibly only partially owns) and controls another company, and this owned company is often referred to as the parent company's subsidiary.

Partial Breach: Where a contracting party fails to meet a term of a contract, but that failure is so minimal that it will not cause a material breach of the contract, nor will it allow the non-breaching party to extricate himself from the contract. This minor breach can often be remedied by the parties through an agreement in which there is a reduction in payment or an adjustment in the performance schedule.

Partial Shipment: Not all the goods being shipped have been received, so the shipment does not constitute fulfillment of the agreement or contract.

Participate: When dealing with business, this refers to making an investment and then receiving a part or share in the ownership, but not necessarily in the management of the organization.

Participation Exemption: Generally the Dutch taxing authorities offer a full exemption from corporate income tax when a corporation owns at least five percent of another company. Essentially a means to prevent double taxation.

Particulars of Claim: In the United Kingdom, this is a document setting out the case of the claimant against the defendant and specifying the facts relied upon.

Partner: One of the individuals in a partnership that is a co-owner and/or an investor in a partnership (which is an on-going business enterprise gone into for profit).

Partnering: An active strategic alliance between two or more companies or individuals to build and expand the operations of both parties to the partnering. Partnering can either be strategic, an on-going relationship, or it can be project specific, meaning limited to one or more specific events.

Partnership: A business enterprise that is for profit and is owned by more than one person, with each being recognized as a partner. Although a partnership can be created orally and with a handshake, often it is formed via a written agreement. Within the partnership, each partner contributes money to the partnership, is responsible for all the debts and contracts of the partnership, has a share in management decisions and shares in profits and losses. One financial key to a partnership is that it does not pay federal or state income taxes, as profits and losses pass through to the individual partners, who report the information on their personal returns (in the United States).

Partnership at Will: A type of partnership where no fixed term has been agreed to for the duration of the partnership. A partnership at will may be dissolved at any time by simply serving notice to the other partner.

Part VI Rules: The collective name for sections of the Financial Services and Markets Act 2000 rules on corporate listing, prospectuses, disclosure and transparency as well as corporate governance.

Part 2 of the Income Tax (Trading and Other Income) Act 2005: This is the statutory provision under which profits from trades and professions are subject to income tax in the United Kingdom.

Part 3 of the Income Tax (Trading and Other Income) Act 2005: This is the provision in the United Kingdom under which individuals are subject to income take for profits from property.

Part 20 Claim: Also known as a third party or counter claim, it can be a counterclaim by a defendant against the claimant and/or a third party; a claim by a defendant against any person for indemnity; and a claim by one third party against another, whether they are party to the suit or not.

Part 36 Offer: This is an offer to settle a claim without prejudice in the United Kingdom. If the offer is not accepted and the one who offers the settlement does better when the case goes to court, the recipient of the offer will see a reduction as to the settlement awarded by the court.

Party: When dealing with contracts, this is an individual or entity that is primarily involved in an agreement with another.

Party of the First Part: This is a reference that identifies one of the parties entering into a written contract with another party (e.g., Cindy Reilly, hereinafter called the party of the first party).

Patent: Granted by the U.S. Patent Office, for example, this provides an exclusive right to the patent owner to all the profits, benefits and uses of his or her invention on the basis that it is novel and useful. Different types of patents (e.g., utility patents or design patents) have protection for different periods of time.

Patent Ambiguity: When dealing with a written document, this represents an obvious inconsistency in its written language.

Patent Claim: Included in a patent application, this is a statement describing, in precise terms, the invention itself, using an established, formal style to put together the description.

Patent Drawing: Included in a patent application, this is a drawing of an invention showcasing all its features, and this is required of all patent applications unless the invention, like a formula, makes a drawing irrelevant.

Patent Pending: This term, often represented as pat. pend. or pat. pending, on a product, is used to put others on notice that an application for a patent has been filed with the U.S. Patent Office, but that a formal patent has yet to be granted.

Patent Infringement: Using, manufacturing, and/or attempting to improve an invention of another-that is patented-without obtaining the patent owner's permission. Whether the infringement is intentional or not, the use of the patented product will cause the illegal user to be liable to the patent owner for all profits made with the product used, as well as any potential harm suffered by the patent owner.

Patent Pool: Three or more parties, each of which has an interest in one or more patents, form an agreement whereby collectively they agree to grant a license or other agreement to a fourth party. The intent in granting the license may be the economic exploitation of all patent holders interests, without the cooperation of all the patent holders, which would otherwise be impossible.

Payable: Meaning a debt which is due to be paid. Although a debt may be owed by an individual or entity, it may not be payable until a certain date or event.

Payable on Demand: When dealing with promissory notes or bills of exchange, this is a debt which must be paid when the person to whom the debt is owed (payee) demands payment on the debt. 2

Payables: The liabilities/debts (short-term) of a business.

Pay as You Earn (PAYE): A system in the United Kingdom whereby employers deduct income tax and national insurance contributions from the employee's gross salary and pay them to HM Revenue & Customs. A similar system exists in the United States.

Payback Period: The amount of time to recover an initial investment; the term of a loan.

Payee: The individual or entity named on a promissory note, check or bill of exchange that will receive payment from the payor.

Payment in Due Course: When money that is due is provided to a holder of a promissory note or bill of exchange without any knowledge that the document had been acquired through fraudulent activities or that the holder of the document does not have valid title to the document. The real owner of the document can demand payment as well, but must get any funds paid from the recipient of the funds.

Payment in Full: Providing all funds due to the individual or entity that is to be the recipient of the funds. Often, this phrase is inserted on the back of a check or on the memo line on the front of a check to show that the cashing or depositing of this document is an acceptance that payment is complete.

Payment into Court: In the United Kingdom, litigation money is paid by or on behalf of a litigant to the Court Funds Office to hold pending resolution of litigation.

Payment of Account: This refers to a partial payment of a debt, usually with an understanding (agreement) that the balance due will be paid at a specified date.

Payor: The party that must make a payment on a promissory note or bill of exchange.

Payroll: A list detailing the people employed by a company and the amount they are due to be paid for their work.

PD Regulations: This is a directive from the European Commission and this regulation specifies the details of the form and content of a prospectus-a document offered by a corporation to potential investors about the financial and other conditions of the company. Investors must receive a prospectus before shares can be sold to them by the issuing company.

Pecuniary: Relating to money.

Peer Review: An evaluation of the performance of an employee by a group of people in the same occupation or with similar skill sets, often in order to assess whether the employee has been properly discharged, denied promotion or overly penalized by an employer

Penalty Clause: Used in contracts, this clause provides that if a party breaks a contract that party is required to pay a penalty (often the penalty is monetary in nature). Often the penalty is a fixed or pre-determined amount.

Pension: A program whereby an employer agrees to provide lifetime benefits for retired workers. A pension may be contributory (where employee and employer make contributions to the plan) and non-contributory. Once an employee has been vested in a pension plan, he retains rights to what has been earned, regardless of his employment status.

Pensions Regulator: Established by the Pensions Act 2004 in the United Kingdom, the regulator has responsibility for all work-based pension schemes. The regulator has the authority to investigate the various pension schemes, issue improvement notices and take action to recover unpaid employer contributions. Essentially the goal is to provide protection for workers covered by the pension schemes.

Peppercorn Rent: In the United Kingdom, this is a token or nominal rent-the name originates from the leases where the rent is one peppercorn a year.

***Per Diem*:** A Latin phrase meaning per day. This term refers to a payment of daily expenses and/or fees accumulated by an employee or agent.

Performance: When dealing with contracts, this is the fulfillment of the obligation of a party to the contract, as required by the terms of the contract. Specific performance of one's obligations to a contract can be demanded in a lawsuit and awarded by the court, forcing the nonperforming party to immediately perform.

Performance Bond: This is essentially a guarantee, a bond designed to ensure that the seller delivers goods or performs a service according to the terms of the contract at the agreed upon time. The bond issuer will pay the buyer a sum of money if he fails to fill the contract as specified.

Period of Incapacity for Work: *See PIW*.

Permanent Establishment: For tax purposes, among others, it is a fixed place of business at which an enterprise is carried on and is the recognized location (in a country) which then taxes the enterprise because it is permanently established in that country. Essentially this avoids double taxation if a company has one or more locations throughout the world.

Per Perocuration: An agent's signature who has only limited authority to sign for his employer or principal. This arrangement is used when frequent signatures are required in the course of business; the principal is liable only to the extent that the agent acts only within his limited authority. A new employee with permission to sign on behalf of the company would never be allowed to sign a major document, an activity for which he was never given permission, oral or written.

Personal Property: All property owned by an individual or entity that does not comprise real estate (property other than land or permanently attached fixtures to the land).

Personal Services: In contract law, these are the unique and special talents of an individual which cannot be performed exactly the same by others. For example, talents of an artist, writer or an actor would fit within this term. This can have strong legal ramifications if the person hired to provide personal services (e.g., a wood sculptor) fails to show up to provide her services, or withdraws from her duties, because she may be liable for damages associated with the difficulty in finding a replacement.

Piece Work: Employees are paid a fixed rate for the units they produce.

Piercing the Corporate Veil: When dealing with corporations, this is a legal response that allows an individual, or individuals, the ability to hold otherwise immune corporate officers and directors personally liable for damages due to the actions of the corporation. The veil represents the immunity of the corporate officers and directors, and it can be pierced when those individuals have acted in an intentional and illegal fashion, or if the powers they have exercised have exceeded those provided by the articles of incorporation. The veil can also be pierced if the corporation is shown to be a completely controlled alter ego (a front company) of another individual or group.

Pilot Operation: A company intends to franchise its business and established a pilot operation, owned by the company, to test the concept and the franchising of its operations. A franchisee could have been recruited on very favorable terms to run a pilot operation with direct assistance from the company.

Pink (Red) Herring: A preliminary prospectus, one that contains most, if not all, of the company information that will be contained in the final prospectus. What is lacking is the number of shares to be offered and the final asking price for the shares. In the United States, it is used as a marketing mechanism for new issues.

PIW: Acronym for period of incapacity for work. PIW is a period of four or more consecutive days during which an employee is incapable of working due to illness.

Plagiarism: Using the written work of another as if it was your own work, and passing it off (selling and/or publishing) to others as if it was in fact your own work. An author of the original work can bring a lawsuit against the plagiarizer to recoup profits made from the plagiarized work.

Plaintiff: The individual or entity that initiates a lawsuit against another party.

Pledge: To promise to do something, or to deposit personal property as security on a loan, and if the loan is not repaid the property is taken to satisfy the debt.

Plus Market: Originally intended to attract smaller companies who were unable or did not wish to pay the costs to be listed on other financial markets, it is basically an off-market share matching and trading facility for buyers and sellers of less-frequently traded stocks.

Poison Pill: A ploy by a company facing a hostile takeover to make their stock appear unattractive and/or inaccessible by offering lower-priced shares to current shareholders in order to make it harder for another company to buy out the company.

Pool: A group of individuals who have organized for the purpose of exploiting certain economic conditions, such as a stock offering or a new venture. The word syndicate is often used as a substitute for pool, e.g. pool of investors.

Pooling: In insurance, companies share premiums and losses among the parties to spread the risks.

Portfolio: The collection or holdings of stocks, bonds and other securities, owned by individuals, corporations or held in trust by a bank or other intermediary. A bank's portfolio might include its entire list of loans outstanding.

Post: In accounting terms, this refers to the recording of a payment.

Postdated: Often done to a check, this refers to writing a future date on a document so that it cannot be transacted before the future date. If the post dated document is a check then it really becomes a promissory note, and if the account to which the check would draw funds is closed or short of funds, the payee, once the check is presented to a bank, has lost rights to demand payment.

Power of Acceptance: The ability to accept an offer, thus creating a binding contract between the parties.

Power of Attorney: A witnessed document allowing the named person to act on behalf of the signator. Power of attorney may be general or for a specific purpose, e.g. signing documents at a loan closing. A durable power of attorney is often used when the person is or remains disabled and cannot mange her affairs.

Practicable: When dealing with contracts, this is when something can be done or performed.

Preemptive Right: A situation where a shareholder in a corporation has the initial chance to purchase a new issue of stock in the corporation, proportionate to the amount he or she already owns.

Preemptory Order: The final order from a governing body or a tribunal which specifies the time and place for compliance. This usually results when one or more parties to an action fail to honor the court's procedural orders. Basically, the court is saying to do something-or else.

Preference: Under bankruptcy law this refers to the payment of debt to a favored creditor as opposed to dividing all assets amongst all those who are owed money-usually this is done just before the debtor files a petition for bankruptcy. This payment to a favored creditor is prohibited by the law, and the payment made must be given to a bankruptcy trustee. This differs from the preference given to creditors with secured debt as approved by a court.

Preferred Dividend: A payment to holders of preferred stock of a corporation's profits.

Preferred Stock: This is a class of shares in a corporation which gives its holders priority in payment of dividends at a fixed rate over those holding common stock. Although seeming to be at an advantage, holders of preferred stock do not partake in higher dividends if the corporation makes a large profit; they cannot vote for directors as does a holder of common stock.

Presentment: When dealing with promissory notes, one makes a demand for payment of the note when it is due.

Prevailing Party: The winner in a lawsuit.

Price Fixing: A criminal violation where two businesses that appear to be in competition reach an agreement for each to set prices for their products, and as a consequence, these set prices prevent actual competition and all the benefits to the public that would have arisen from the competition. In addition, it is also a price fixing violation if suppliers and manufactures (or distributors) secretly set favorable prices to beat competition. This act violates the antitrust laws.

Principal: Often an employer, this is an individual who is responsible for hiring and directing employees (agents), and who may ultimately be responsible for the acts done by these employees for his or her benefit. *See* ***respondent superior***.

Principal Place of Business: The geographical location of a businesses home/head office where books, records, contracts and other important documents are kept, and often where senior management works. Most states require businesses to report their principal place of business to the Secretary of State

Principal Register: When dealing with both trademarks and service marks, this is a list to which those marks that are approved for federal regulation are placed.

Priority: When dealing with bankruptcy law, this is the right given to taxing authorities, judgment holders, secured creditors, bankruptcy trustees and attorneys to collect before general creditors are able to collect.

Privacy Laws: Statues that forbid an invasion of an individual's right to privacy and restricts access to personal data, including health care information, under many circumstances.

Private Carrier: Someone that, for just a particular instance, provides transportation or delivery of goods for money, but not as a regular business dealing.

Privitization: An action to sell government-owned or government-subsidized business and operations to the public as stock companies, to be managed by professionals from within the industry for the future profit of the new shareholders. A general tendency to get government out of directly managing businesses.

Privity: A direct, mutual relationship and/or interest between parties (e.g., such as a relationship between a consumer and a retailer). When dealing with contracts, there must be privity for one party to enforce a contract by a lawsuit against the other party.

Process Server: A person that delivers legal documents to another in lawsuits. This can be done either by a professional server or a government official, such as a deputy sheriff.

Product Liability: The responsibility of manufacturers, distributors and sellers of products to the public to make certain that its products are free of defects that can potentially cause harm, and if these products do make their way to the marketplace, to have them removed or to replace the defective products or pay for any harm suffered as a result of these products.

Productivity: The rise (or fall) of the output of workers and business assets to units produced. In a service business, productivity may be measured by the number of customer service phone calls taken or stocks sold. Productivity is a measure of increased activity using the same resources: workers, fixed assets, machinery and computers.

Profit and Loss Statement: Based on a company's current operations, this is a document detailing the profits or losses with regards to a company's sales.

***Pro Forma*:** A Latin phrase meaning as a matter of form. In accounting, this phrase refers to an accountant's proposed financial statement for a business (based upon an assumption that certain events will occur), like an increase in inflation.

Pro Rata: A Latin phrase meaning in proportion. This refers to an amount to be paid or a share to be received, and this is based upon the fractional or proportional share of ownership and/or responsibility.

Promise: When dealing with contracts, a promise exchanged by both parties is consideration for the promise, and a failure to fulfill one's promise will be cause for breach of the contract.

Promissory Note: This is a written document by an individual (often referred to as the maker or payor) whereby he or she promises to pay a specified amount of money on a specified date to another (referred to as the payee). These notes also often include a specified amount of interest to be paid if payment on the note goes unpaid. The time of payment varies, and it may be on a specific date, due in installments or on demand.

Promoter: An individual that is tasked with putting together a corporation by helping with the initial financing. Often this individual is the principal shareholder or one of the key managers of the business, and he or she justifies the shareholding (promotional stock given to him or her) primarily on the basis of his or her efforts to help build the company and attract investors. Most states limit the amount of promotional stock because it is based upon effort and not assets and/or cash invested.

Promotional Stock: These are the shares issued when a corporation is newly formed, and these shares are given to the promoter as payment for his or her efforts in helping to form and organize the business, and also because he or she helps line up investors and/or other potential shareholders. Most states limit the amount of promotional stock because it is based upon effort and not assets and/or cash.

Property: The right to possession, enjoyment or disposition of all things, subject to proof of ownership. Property can be real (land and buildings) or personal (everything else that is not considered real property).

Proprietary Interest: Ownership, either in total or partial form.

Proprietary Rights: These are the rights that go with the ownership of real estate and/or a business.

Proprietor: Although this means the owner of anything, it is most often referring to the owner/operator of a business.

Prospectus: Offered by a corporation, this detailed document is issued to potential shareholders highlighting the corporation's past and present performance and its prospects. It includes the financial status, the officers, the plans, recent performance and other matters which would assist the potential investor in evaluating the stock and the prospects of the company for profit, loss or growth. The Federal Securities Act requires that a prospectus be filed with the Securities and Exchange Commission (SEC) and that the Commission grant approval before any major share issue occurs. State laws generally require similar documentation.

Protectionism: Specific government policy (or political pressure) to safeguard a local producer from competition from a foreign producer. Tariffs are often placed on goods or services from foreign countries to make them less competitive to local producers. In an era of increasingly open markets, protectionism is difficult to enforce without retaliation. Protectionism can take on more subtle forms, such as government subsidies or grants.

Provision/Proviso: This refers to a condition or term within a contract.

Proxy: An individual given the authority to serve in another's place at a meeting, and often given the right to vote for the person he or she is representing at the meeting. (This also refers to the written authority allowing this action.) Often, a proxy is given to go to a shareholder's meeting with the task of casting a shareholder's vote.

Prudent Man Rule: The legal application of prudence, whereby an action taken would be done or not done judged on what other, prudent men would do. As an officer of a company with responsibility for a pension plan or other retirement system, the prudent man rule would prevent investing in speculative securities or businesses which might jeopardize the financial future of the plan. The same principle would apply to someone who manages a trust or estate.

Public Corporation: This refers to a corporation that operates under government control, or one that is created to perform a governmental task (e.g., a hospital).

Public Domain: A right which allows anyone, without permission from a works owner, to use creative work, an invention or logo, often because patent, trademark and copyright protection has expired (e.g., the works of William Shakespeare may be published by anyone without paying a royalty).

Puffing: When one grossly exaggerates the value and/or usefulness of a product, business, etc., in order to make a sale. These types of outlandish lies or exaggerations can be the basis for a lawsuit if the exaggeration exceeds the reality.

Punitive Damages: In a lawsuit, these are the damages awarded to the prevailing party as punishment for the malicious or fraudulent acts of the losing party.

Q

Qard: A loan under Islamic tradition.

Qard Hasan: A benevolent loan for social welfare; it is an interest-free loan to individuals in need.

QCA: *See **Quoted Companies Alliance***

QCA Guidelines: Any company listed on the Alternative Investment Market (AIM) would be required to follow the corporate governance guidelines published by the Quoted Companies Alliance (QCA) of 2005.

QIB: *See **qualified institutional buyer**.*

Qualified Institutional Buyer (QIB): Typically, these are institutions that own and invest on a discretionary basis at least US$100 million of securities; the group might also include banks and investment companies. Registered dealers, unlike institutions, are required to have US$10 million invested on a discretionary basis.

Qualified Opinion: Such a statement is issued by an auditor when the company's financial position and statements, as a result of operations, are in conformity to generally accepted accounting principles (GAAP) with an exception (or more than one exception). The auditor would then write in detail about the exceptions to standard practice in more detail.

Qualifying Disclosure: In the United Kingdom under the Public Interest Disclosure Act 1998 this is a protected disclosure, e.g. information provided under the whistle-blowing legislation designed to protect the sources of such information. Similar laws and regulations exist in the United States.

Qualifying Employee Share Ownership Trust (QUEST): Employee share trusts are discretionary, for the benefit of employees. Typically the trust is composed of shares of the issuing company; in some cases there can be favorable tax treatment of this trust in the United Kingdom.

Qualifying Investments: All financial instruments as defined under the context of the market abuse directive: for example, shares (stocks) in companies, bonds, money market instruments, financial futures, forward contracts, options, derivatives on commodities, swaps of all kinds and any instrument traded on a regulated market or exchange.

Qualifying Period: Under employment law in the United Kingdom, the period of time employees would have worked continuously for an employer in order to be eligible for certain rights and benefits-for example, one year to claim unfair dismissal. Different benefits and rights have different qualifying periods.

Quantitative Restrictions: Government or other regulating body's limits on the number of goods or the value of goods which may be imported into a country at one time or over a period of time.

Quantity Controls: Government or other regulating body's limits on the amount of foreign exchange that may be paid out for a purchase of goods or services. This is used particularly in countries with weak currencies in an attempt to hold on to hard currency: dollar, yen, euros, etc.

Quantum Meruit: This Latin phrase means as much as he deserved, and it refers to and helps determine the amount that is to be paid for services when no contract was entered into by two parties, or if there is some doubt as to the amount due for services performed.

Quarter Days: In the United Kingdom, Wales and Ireland they are traditionally the four days marking the beginning of each quarter of the year: March 25th, June 24th, September 29th and December 24th. They are traditionally days for settling debts, rents for example. These are no longer fixed dates, as local authorities often use January 1st, April 1st, July 1st and October 1st rather than the traditional days.

Quashing Order: Also know as certiorari, a judicial remedy that quashes the decision in question.

Queen's Bench: In the United Kingdom this is the highest court of the land during the reign of a Queen. Opinions proffered by this court are identified as a volume of Queen's Bench (QB).

QUEST: *See **qualifying employees share ownership trust**.*

Quid pro Quo: This Latin phrase means something for something and is often used in contractual dealings under the phrase mutual consideration; it refers to and identifies what each party to an agreement expects from the other.

Quorum: Often used in business settings, this refers to the number of individuals mandated to be present before a meeting can be opened to conduct business. Usually this number of individuals equals a majority of members. For example, at a meeting of the board of directions, there needs to be a quorum of directors present to act or otherwise authorize action on behalf of the board and the company.

Quoted Companies Alliance (QCA): An organization in the United Kingdom who role is to manage the interests of smaller companies quoted on the London Stock Exchange, e.g. companies outside of the FTSE 350.

R

Race Discrimination Questionnaire (RR65): In the United Kingdom, this questionnaire is used by those who believe that they have been discriminated on the basis of race; it is a means to serve notice to the alleged discriminator. The goal is to gather information to determine whether a proceeding should be bought before the employment tribunal.

Race Relations Act: *See RRA.*

Rack Rent: The full open market value of a holding; what the market would bear in terms of rental income.

Rahm: In Islamic finance, this is collateral for a debt or loan.

Raider: In business takeovers, an unfriendly or unwanted suitor who is interested in acquiring a majority of another company.

Random Walk: A general principle of students of the financial markets which suggests that price fluctuations of stocks and other securities are random, meaning that their direction from one time to another is unpredictable. This theory is closely related to the efficient market hypothesis.

RAPES System: An emergency notification system used in the E.U. whereby member states notifies the European Commission when they discover a product in their market that poses a serious risk to members and to consumers. It is a rapid exchange information system.

Rate Cap: A limit as to the amount of interest that can be charged on a loan; this is particularly important in adjustable-rate loans and mortgages. Rate caps prevent the interest on a mortgage from skyrocketing in a time of generally high interest rates or when inflation is prevalent. This can be an important contractual item in consumer and business lending.

Rate Scale: In business, publishing the terms of your services or products; rates can be based on weight, units, distance or geographic zone in shipping, for example. A rate scale, once published without qualification, implies a contract.

Ratification: Often seen in principal/agent (employer/employee) law, this is a situation when an employee acts in a fashion that was not pre-approved or possibly not even authorized by the company, but his or her acts have been adopted by the employer. In short, the actions are approved by the principal/employer in their name after the fact.

Rating Agency: Groups such as Moody's, Fitch or Standard & Poor's, they are organizations specializing in evaluating the financial well-being of companies and their securities. Typically, they assign a credit rating to a firm's bonds, for example. Rating agencies can have a direct bearing on a company's cost when borrowing money. The higher the rating, the lower the interest rate charged. Unrated corporate bonds are considered junk and are highly risky for investors to include in an investment portfolio.

Ratings: Overall, a grade or classification-could be credit, quality of bonds, profitability of a business or creditworthiness of an individual. Typically, ratings are systematic and highly analytical tools.

Ratio: A mathematical relationship between one variable and another. Ratios are a version of shorthand which helps investors, manager and lenders understand quickly and efficiently how the items compare. They are neither detailed nor should they be used out of context. There are literally hundreds of financial ratios used in business-sales to profits, assets to liabilities and so forth. A ratio by itself tells little except as a general indicator of the condition being analyzed.

Readily Convertible Assets: Generally speaking, assets which are easily traded or converted to cash such as stocks, bonds or precious metals. Readily convertible assets are similar to short-term assets, e.g. meaning that they can be liquidated within one year.

Readjustment: While it has various meanings, generally it is a period of time after a recession or financial panic at which time business and finance returns to a more normal state. For example, the real estate market has readjusted to a period of high interest rates and activity within the market has increased to previous year (periods) level.

Real Estate: Real property such as lands, buildings and improvements which are permanently attached. Often it is classified as rural, farm or urban.

Real Property: As opposed to personal property, this is land and any buildings or other attachments, including landscaping, on the land. An owner of real property has all the rights, benefits and interests in the same property and can dispose of it or not as he sees fit.

Realization: Converting non-cash resources and rights into money. Accrual accounting recognizes revenue only when it has been earned, e.g. realized.

Reasonable Adjustment: In the United Kingdom, based on the Disability Discrimination Act 1995, employers are required to make reasonable work place adjustments for the handicapped or disabled. Similar laws exist in the United States and most advanced economies. For example, a shorter desk or work table or better lighting might be added. The general assumption is that the adjustment is one that will not cost the employer a great deal of money, thus the accommodation is reasonable.

Reasonable Reliance: Often seen when dealing with contracts, this is what one party (a prudent person) would believe or feel secure in acting upon based on a promise, and as such, acts upon that promise and finds out he or she has been misled. If this reliance was reasonable, then the acting party can seek and recover damages or can require the contract to be enforced.

Reasonable Search: Under most civil proceedings, parties to the action are not obligated to conduct an exhaustive search for all and every so-called relevant document; rather the court will accept a reasonable search, the rules of which are contingent upon the civil proceedings. The definition of reasonable search will vary depending upon the proceedings and the complexity of the case.

Rebate: This often refers to money returned to a buyer based on a discount on a product; or this can be money returned because a buyer paid too much. Rebates are often used as incentives to buy, especially large-ticket items such as cars or even houses (in a slow real estate market). Even smaller consumer products will offer rebates which require the consumer to take very specific actions in order to receive the benefit of the offer.

Recapitalization: A voluntary change in the capital structure of a business-one that is not ordered by the courts, such as through bankruptcy. Simple decisions to offer more shares for sale to the public or to go from a privately-held company to a publicly-held company are examples of recapitalization.

Receipt: A written document that provides a buyer with proof of purchase and/or that he or she has paid for the goods or paid a debt. A receipt is generally good business and consumer practice when a transaction is paid for in cash.

Receiver: Appointed by the courts, this individual takes charge of the assets or property of a debtor in order to preserve as much of the assets on behalf of the creditor(s) as possible. The duties are custodial in nature. A receiver is often used in bankruptcy proceedings.

Reciprocity: In general, any mutual exchange of rights or privileges. In international business, two countries allow businesses from the other to operate in their countries on roughly the same and equal footing, including protection under the laws of each country.

Record Date: In the United Kingdom, the date on which a shareholder must officially own shares to be entitled to a dividend.

Recourse: The right of the individual in possession of a check or bill of exchange to demand payment from the writer of the document.

Recovery Plan: In the United Kingdom, based on the Pensions Act 2004, the trustees of a salary-related pension scheme must agree to make up any short-fall and eliminate any deficit in the plan. Typically, the employer will be responsible for making the plan whole. The recovery plan must be very specific and to when and how much will be paid.

Rectification: Basically, correcting the mistakes made in written contracts; one party to the contract must prove convincingly that the current document does not reflect the intentions of the parties to the agreement, and thus needs to be rectified. This can be difficult, but other documents, correspondence and transcripts or details of conversations (witnesses) may be enough for rectification.

Recusal: Whether by his own volition or by petition of one or other parties in a proceedings, the judge will step down from the case because of a real or perceived conflict of interest.

Red Circle: In the United Kingdom, this is the practice of freezing an employee's pay because she is paid more that other workers doing essentially the same work. The pay is frozen until such a time that others catch up. This can happen in reorganizations or when a company is sold.

Red Clause Letter of Credit: At times a letter of credit will contain a clause, traditionally printed in red, authorizing a bank to pay on the letter of credit before the shipment arrives or before all the documents have been presented and processed. Although unusual, buyers may want from time to time to make such concessions in order to further a business relationship.

Redact: Literally, the word means to edit. Confidential information may be blacked out in the course of litigation or blocked from readers in the course of an acquisition, say before a confidentiality agreement is signed. Generally, the purpose is to protect the document owner from disclosing information either not needed or not requiring disclosure.

Redemptions: Payment of a debt or the retirement of a bond issue by paying the bond holders in full; cancellation of a debt. The bonds are said to be redeemed when paid.

Redeployment: Typically in the United Kingdom an employee is moved to a different department or even a different subsidiary; this is used to avoid firing an employee because of redundancy. The employment contract will have to be changed as a result, which means that this can only be done with the employee's consent.

Redlining: Refusing to grant loans in certain neighborhoods or districts, regardless of the quality of the security or the ability of the borrower to repay the loan. Redlining generally is illegal. Redlining can also apply to such transactions as house or property insurance. In most cases, it is seen a form of discrimination because it assume a whole class (neighborhood) cannot repay or are not insurance worthy.

Redundancy: Basis for termination of employment because the employee's position no longer exists or is needed. In the United Kingdom, there is a very specific process for handling redundancies; other countries are less strict.

Re-engagement Order: In the United Kingdom, an employment tribunal will issue an order that an employer must re-employ a dismissed worker on new terms and without loss of continuity of employment. The assumption is that the employee fired was done so unjustly or incorrectly.

Refinance: To pay off one loan with another one; this is frequently used for mortgages, student loans or credit card debt when interest rates go down. The value of refinancing to consumer and companies is dependent on any fees attached to refinancing, limitations on early payoff in a contract (a penalty if paid off before the due date) and the amount that interest rates go down.

Reformation: A court modification of contractual terms when the court feels that the agreement did not reflect the true intent of both parties.

Regional Development Agencies: In the United Kingdom there are nine of these bodies whose primary purpose is to assist in regional economic development.

Regional Spatial Strategies: In the United Kingdom, the Regional Assembly, based on national policy, co-ordinates the use and development of land.

Register: Within corporations, this is the record of the corporation's shareholders, as well as the issuance and transfer of its shares.

Registration Statement: This is a written document prepared by a corporation and filed with the Securities and Exchange Commission (SEC) that details an issuance of shares to be sold to the general public. This report must be approved by the SEC before any stock can be issued and sold.

Regulated Activity: In the United Kingdom, any business activity that falls under the jurisdiction of the Financial Services and Markets Act 2000. Regulated activities include such activities as deposits in a bank, insurance contracts or investment activities.

Regulation FD: Under the fair disclosure requirements of the Securities and Exchange Commission (SEC) in the United States, it prohibits disclosure of non-public investment information to securities industry professionals or institutional investors who might be expected to trade on this information (to their benefit) and the detriment of the general investing public.

Regulation S: Under the United States Securities Act of 1933, it provides a safe harbor from registration requirements and sales of securities outside the U.S., assuming certain conditions are met.

Rehypothecate: To pledge collateral a second time. A bank holds stock as collateral for a loan and then pledges the same stock as collateral for a loan from another bank. This can only be done with the customer's consent, as the customer still owns the pledged security.

Reinstatement: In business labor law, for example, a dismissed employee is returned to his former position at the same salary and with the same benefits before a temporary layoff or planned termination. Reinstatement could result from a variety of reason, not the least is human error.

Reinsurrance: To mitigate all or part of the risk, an insurance company will assign part of the coverage (for a premium) to another insurer. This is often used in large, risky or complicated insurance transactions and is used as a prudent means of lessening risk. Some kinds of insurance companies are incorporated solely for the purpose of reinsurance.

Release: When dealing with contracts, this means to give up a right. For example, allowing another party to forego his or her obligation to perform under a contract.

Reliance Loss: As opposed to expectation loss (the normal assessment of damages for breach of contract), this is the ability to recover losses as though the contract had never happened. The goal is to prevent unjust impoverishment. A claimant cannot recover both expectation loss as well as reliance loss.

Relief from Forfeiture: In the United Kingdom, a landlord seeks relief and wants to terminate a lease because of a breach of agreement by the tenant. The tenant has a right to petition the court for relief, providing he acts quickly and pays all arrears and/or remedies any other breaches in the agreement.

Remoteness: Used to determine an award of damages in a contract situation, the claimant will be able to recover losses either naturally arising from the breach or any loss that may be reasonably supposed to have been contemplated by the parties to the agreement in the even of a breach of contract.

Remuneration: What an employer is to pay an employee under terms of an employment agreement or contract. Benefits, reimbursed expenses or tips by a third party are not typically considered remuneration.

Renegotiate: In law or business, changing or modifying an oral or written provision to a valid, legally binding contract.

Renewal: To keep in effect an existing arrangement for an additional, often set, period of time. This action usually requires a writing evidencing the new term or time period.

Reopener Clause: An allowance in a contract for an item or items in the contract to be reopened or renegotiated, provided that certain conditions anticipated by the contract take place.

Reorganization: A term utilized when a corporation makes plans to restructure, which often includes transfers of shares between shareholders of two corporations, which usually leads to a merger. If a corporation is in the throws of bankruptcy due to financial trouble, a bankruptcy court may provide time for the corporation to reorganize to protect it from creditors, with the hope it can pay creditors once reorganized.

Repatriation: Returning to the host country profits, assets, personnel or equipment used in a foreign country. In an effort to boost investment in some countries, they make repatriation of profits very easy for companies who open operations in these countries.

Replevin: Although not used in most states, this was a common law rule which provided a right to the owner of goods that were improperly taken by another to bring a lawsuit to recover the goods.

Repossess: Where property is taken back by a seller, by judicial processes or self-help, because the buyer has breached a contract in some form or another. Cars are frequently repossessed without court permission by the lender when consumers fail to make payments.

Repudiation: Where one party to a contract refuses to honor his or her obligations to the contract, effectuating an anticipatory breach of the contract.

Repudiatory Breach: A fundamental breach of contract by either the employee or the employer which entitles either part to terminate the relationship without giving notice.

Requirements Contract: This is an agreement between a supplier of goods and a buyer, in which the supplier agrees to sell all of a particular kind of goods the buyer needs, and the buyer in turn agrees to buy exclusively these particular goods from the supplier. This differs from an output contract, because in that particular agreement the buyer agrees to buy everything produced by the supplier.

Res Judicata: A Latin term short for, *res judicata pro veritate accipitur*. Essentially, the principal that a decision by a judge is conclusive between two parties to an action.

Reschedule: A willingness on the part of a lender to change the schedule of debt payments of the debtor, often when the debtor's financial position is deteriorating. Rescheduling debt is an attempt to keep the debtor out of bankruptcy and prevent a loan from being written off.

Rescission: Where both parties to a contract, by mutual agreement or judicial order, agree to cancel the contract and return to the relationship they had before entering into the contract.

Research and Development Agreement: An exception to most regulations prohibiting restrain of trade or monopolies, competitors may enter into a research and development agreement in order to develop a new technology or product. The expectation is that they will share the costs of development and also enjoy the benefits of the research in proportion to the costs paid by each party. These kinds of agreements are not, in the spirit of the law, intended to limit competition. In reality, they are often used for large-scale or expensive research efforts, new drugs or some kind of sophisticated technology where neither of the parties can afford to assume all the costs and thus all the risk.

Respondent: In the United Kingdom, it is the company or organization against which a claim is made in an employment tribunal.

Respondent Superior: A Latin term meaning, let the master answer. An important term within the confines of business and agency law, this refers to the relationship of the agent (employee) and the principal (employer). It dictates that a principal is responsible for the actions of its agents when those actions are done within the scope of employment, and as such, an agent may be able to bind a principal to contracts or other written and verbal agreements made on its behalf.

Restitution: One party makes a claim that the other party was unjustly enriched at his expense. Restitution is provided to make the first party whole, by making good the loss that he suffered.

Restraint of Trade: When dealing with antitrust law, this would be any activity that has the effect of limiting trade, sales and transportation in interstate commerce. Most antitrust statutes make these types of actions illegal.

Restrictive Covenant: A provision in an employment contract prohibiting a former employee from certain post-employment activities-generally activities which would materially harm the former employee. An example might be that upon termination, a former employee may not work for certain close competitors for a period of time. To be effective, a restrictive covenant has to be reasonable, e.g. not barring employment with a competitor for an excessive length of time.

Restrictive Endorsement: An endorsement (signature) which places a restriction on to whom a document, such as a check, note or bill of exchange, may be transferred too. For example, a check may read, for transfer only to Annabelle Otto, [signed] Michelle Otto.

Retaliation: In business, simply giving back punishment of equal kind; one country retaliates by increasing tariffs on products from another country who had just raised its tariffs.

Retainer: The engagement and payment of a lawyer, barrister or solicitor or other expert to defend a party in an action or to advise a party, whether there is legal action involved or not.

Retention: In the course of an acquisition of one company by another, part of the purchase price may be held back by the buyer in anticipation of some kind of breach or other problem, e.g. the assets sold or the businesses as presented at the time of sale were not accurate or fully accounted for. Retention can be used to ensure that there are not undisclosed debts or that there is a pending lawsuit which would materially affect the value of the business or assets as purchased.

Retire: In finance this refers to when a promissory note is paid off, effectively retiring the loan.

Reverse Surrender: A tenant gives up a lease, in effect pays the landlord to accept the surrender. Basically, buying out of a lease, often at a premium.

Reverse Takeover: The somewhat unusual circumstance in which the buyer, for example, is actually smaller than the company being bought; in the normal course of business, it is assumed that larger companies buy smaller organizations, not the reverse.

Revocation: In contractual law, this refers to a situation where both parties agree mutually to cancel a contract. It also refers to a situation where one party withdraws his or her offer before it is accepted by another party

Revolving Credit: Often called a revolving loan, a credit that is renewed or reinstated without specific written documents amending the original loan agreement.

Riba: Under Islamic law, this is interest or an unjust return on a business transaction and is forbidden.

Riba al Diyun: Usury in pre-Islamic law; an amount added to a debt (principal). A means of avoiding interest which is illegal.

Rider: This is a written document attached to an existing document (for example, when language is added to an insurance policy) and it serves to amend or add to the existing document. The full terms of the agreement, then, are contained in the original document and the added pages (rider).

Right of Pre-emption: Simply, the right of first refusal by which the seller by agreement offers a property to a buyer before all other buyers, for example. The potential buyer has the right to refuse the offer.

Right of Redemption: By paying a delinquent debt, the borrower has the right to recover personal or real property that was transferred to another because of a lien.

Risk: The degree that an expected return on an investment will be different than anticipated. There are a variety of investment and business risks which may affect the outcome: interest rate risk, market risk, inflation risk, business risk, financial risk and liquidity risk.

Robert Morris Associates: An association of bank and loan officers whose function is to conduct research and track trends in bank lending and credit. One of the key measures published monthly is the number of loans in default.

Rollover: A refinancing arrangement whereby with the permission of the bank, a borrower postpones payment on the loan and seeks to reorganize the entire loan.

Root of Title: In the United Kingdom, this is the deed to which title to a property is traced to prove that the owner has a good title. This situation applies only to unregistered land. In order to register the land, there has to be a string of unbroken titles/ownership going back at least 15 years.

Royalty: This is a monetary amount, often based on a percentage of gross revenues, paid to an author or creator; it is based upon a calculation of the proportion of money received from the sale of the product. Usually the terms of the amount to be paid are found within a contract between the parties. Royalties can be paid on books, software, recordings, movies, television properties and a host of technologies and inventions.

RRA: Acronym for the Race Relations Act 1976 which prohibits discrimination based on color, race, nationality, ethnic or national origin. Generally covers employment, services and housing.

Rule 10b: Disclosure Letter: Under the U.S. Securities and Exchange Act of 1934, liability will be attached if the offering documents lack material or significant information which may mislead or otherwise contains untrue statements about the offering. Typically a letter is from the lawyers stating that they have done due diligence in this matter.

Russian Roulette: One shareholder to a joint venture serves notice by offering to transfer all if his shares in the venture to the partner at a specified price. The second party must accept the offer and buy at the stated price or its must sell to the first part at the same price per share. In either case, the intent is to terminate the joint venture, one way or the other.

S

Safe Harbour: In the United Kingdom, this is a category of investment behavior which can never amount to market abuse under U.K. rules.

Salaried Partner: Generally a hired manager of partner status; although a partner, she has no right to share in the profits (or losses for that matter) and has no voting rights in terms of the overall company.

Sale: An act whereby the seller of goods or services transfers said goods or services to a buyer in exchange for something (most often money). The price paid by the buyer to the seller may be listed or announced, or it can be established by negotiation or bidding at an auction.

Sale and Leaseback: This strategy often is used to increase cash flow and make better use of available assets. Company A sells its headquarters to an investment group, who then turns around and leases the building back to Company A. The company, as a result of the transaction, has a large source of capital to pay down debt or invest in its business without interrupting its daily business with the effort to find a new offices, thus not forced to move employees and equipment. The leaseback is generally agreed to before the sale, so the terms are consistent with company's expectations and cash flow.

SAMREC: Acronym for the South African Code for Mineral Resources and Mineral Reserves. This is a document published under the auspices of the South African Mineral committee to track mineral reserves and mining activity in a country where mining is a huge, dominant industry.

Samurai Bonds: Foreign bonds denominated in Japanese yen.

Sarbane-Oxley Act of 2002: This act is the most important corporate reporting change in decades; it is designed to ensure that the accounting profession and senior management take full responsibility for the accuracy of the financial information issued to the public. The corporate governance and disclosure changes are a result for scandals in the United States, such as Enron and Tyco.

Satisfaction: Where a party receives payment that is due, or if dealing with a contract, performance that is due.

Satisfactory Quality: In the United Kingdom, under the Sale of Goods Act 1979, goods are of satisfactory quality if they meet the standards which a reasonable person would set. It is an implied term in a contract for the sale of goods. Some of the standards might include: durability, no minor defects, quality of the appearance and the finish of the product and that the goods do/are what they are supposed to do/be.

SAYE Option Scheme: This is a kind of employee share scheme used in the United Kingdom. Employees can be offered as much as a 20 percent discount on the options, but all employees must be able to participate-after having qualified based on a number of years of service. The plan is linked to a savings account to pay for the shares.

Schedule A: Non-capital expenditures of a business nature, such as rents, advertising and repairs for the sake of reporting income taxes in the United Kingdom.

Schedule of Dilapidations: A term used in the United Kingdom for those items in need of repair which are the responsibility of the tenant, based on a lease signed by the landlord and the tenant. A landlord has the right to submit a list (schedule) of needed repairs to the tenant, usually at the end of the lease.

Scheme Actuary: In the United Kingdom, an occupational pension scheme must have an actuary appointed to advise the trustees of the pension scheme. The actuary must be an individual, not a firm, and she must be a fellow of the Faculty and Institute of Actuaries.

Scheme of Arrangement: In the United Kingdom, this is a compromise between a company and its creditors. Under this arrangement, a company can put together almost any kind of plan-reorganization, merger or demerger. The plan must be approved by at least ¾ of the creditors. The scheme also has to be approved by shareholders.

Scheme Rescue: In the United Kingdom this occurs when a company which has an occupational pension scheme is insolvent and another company, either a buyer of the insolvent company or other group, takes over responsibility for funding the pension scheme.

Scope of Employment: This refers to those actions by an employee that are done in furtherance of the business of his or her employer, as opposed to actions done by the employee while doing his or her own personal business. This distinction is important as far as any potential liability imputing to the employer is concerned, because if the acts of an employee while working are outside the scope of his or her employment the employer might be seen as not liable for the employee's acts. If he or she is within the scope of their employment when an accident occurs, then this might be imputed to the employer under the doctrine of respondent superior.

Scrivener: An individual that, for a fee, writes out a document for another (can be several types of written documents).

SDA: Acronym for the Sex Discrimination Act 1975 which prohibits discrimination based on gender or marital status in employment and when offering a contract for employment.

Secondment Agreement: In the United Kingdom if an employee is transferred temporarily from one organization to another for a limited period of time (usually to complete a specific project or assignment), this agreement will detail the responsibilities of all parties concerned. In most cases, the employee remains with the company that did the transferring and it would continue to pay employee salary and benefits.

Section 146 Notice: Under the Law of Property Act 1925 in the United Kingdom, a notice is issued by the landlord that the tenant is in breach of the lease and that the intent is to cancel the lease unless the tenant can and does rectify the breach (often through a cash payment to the landlord).

Section 212 Notice: Under the Companies Act 1985 public companies in the United Kingdom are allowed to investigate any individuals interested in or who has been acquiring its shares. This allows the company to identify any potential predators in the works. This section was replaced and rewritten in 2007.

Section 793 Notice: Related to Section 212 Notice above, this allows U. K. companies to require any person who has interest in or is acquiring its shares to either confirm or deny the facts and give information about their intent in acquiring company shares.

Secured Debt: When a creditor has a lien on a debt, allowing the creditor to bring an action for repossession or foreclosure, where default occurs, in order to take the property secured by the lien.

Secured Transaction: Where property is pledged as security on a loan or credit to protect the lender in case payment is not made.

Securities: A generic term, these are financial instruments issued by corporations (e.g., shares of stock, bonds, debentures) traded on a stock exchange and that produce an income. The term securities is derived from the fact that the assets and/or the profits of the corporation or the credit of the government stand as security for payment, but because no property is pledged, securities are dependant on the future profitability of the corporation.

Securities Act of 1933: Securities law in the United States which regulates the offer and sales of all securities by an issuer to the public. The securities must be registered and a prospectus is required when offering stock to the public.

Securities Exchange Act of 1934: Securities law in the United States which regulates the trading of securities of public companies; the over all goals are to prevent fraud and to ensure that the public is protected. Brokers and dealers must also register with the Securities and Exchange Commission (SEC).

Securitization: Credit card loans, student loans, mortgages and accounts receivables are packaged and sold as securities to investors. Securitization has the benefit of making financial institutions liquid in that when they sell their loans to investors, they have new cash with which to lend. Almost any assets that have a predicable cash flow can be securitized.

Security of Costs: In the United Kingdom, an order is given which requires one part to pay money (or offer a bond) to the court as security for their opponents costs. This ensures that if a claimant wins and the other party is ordered to pay court costs, the money is available to the winning side.

Selective Distribution: A distribution system which limits the number of distributors handling a line of goods; these distributors must meet certain standards (financial and otherwise) and must agree to limit their sales to approved vendors, who also meet certain standards.

Self-dealing: Using privileged inside information attained by being an official of a corporation (or from an officer or official of a corporation) in order to buy or sell stock before the information (e.g., a merger) is made public. A general partner of a limited partnership can also be accused of self-dealing if he or she does not inform limited partners of business opportunities that belong to the partnership. Self-dealing can result in a lawsuit for fraud by shareholders. These types of actions are crimes under the Securities and Exchange Act.

Sensitive Personal Data: This can include court, health, employment or credit information about individuals-race, national origin, mental or physical health, financial data or other information to which an individual has an expectation of privacy.

Servant: When dealing in agency and business law, this is an employee under the direction and control of an employer (master), and he or she has duties and obligations under the employer's authority.

Service Mark: Used by businesses to differentiate and identify its services from those offered by its competitors, this mark is often in the form of a logo, symbol, phrase or word, and is distinguishable from a trademark which is used to identify a product.

Set-off: A cross-claim by a debtor against a creditor which would reduce the creditor's claim by the amount of the cross-claim. There are four types: legal set-off, equitable set-off, banker's set-off and insolvency set-off.

SETS: Acronym for the Stock Exchange Electronic Trading Service in the United Kingdom. It is the central trading book and trading mechanism for the securities comprising the FTSE 100 Index. Members can enter, buy or sell shares and they will be matched electronically with corresponding parties.

Severable Contract: This is a type of agreement between parties in which there are a number of separate contracts between the parties allowing for a breach of one of the separate elements without breaching the remainder of the overall contract. Therefore, severing a part of this type of agreement will not excuse the other party from honoring those other contract parts that have not been breached. For example, if a movie theater contracts with a vendor to deliver all popcorn, candy and cups-each with separate prices-but later the vendor no longer makes cups and cannot deliver them, the other deliverable goods within the different parts of the contract remain in force between the parties.

Severability Clause: A section within a contract which allows for the preservation of a portion of a contract if other parts are invalidated by a court.

Several Liability: Two parties assume liability, each of them is treated as having assumed liability only for its portion of what is due; in effect, each party is solely responsible for its own failure to perform and not the other party's failure to perform.

Severance Agreement: A written record of any employee's departure from an employer and what, if any, benefits he may be entitled to. These agreements are often written with the understanding that the employee will waive any and all future claims against the employer. This is an important mechanism to prevent lawsuits from former employees.

Severance Pay: Money paid to an employee laid-off from his or her position within a company (not necessarily fired). Although not a requirement, if offered in a contract it must be paid.

Share: In business relations, this represents a portion of ownership of a corporation, and is represented by a stock certificate that details the number of stocks owned.

Share (Stock) Buyback: A company goes to the open market or to large holders of its stocks and buys the shares back, thus becoming treasury stock. This reduces the number of shares available to the public and generally is done as a means to increase the price of the stock. Buybacks are common when directors feel that the stock price is depressed for no good business reason and to reward current shareholders with an increased stock price.

Shareholder: This is the owner of one or more shares of a corporation, and is often referred to as a stockholder. A shareholder has rights conferred by the bylaws of a corporation, as well as those provided by law. Also, a shareholder, among others, has the right to vote at meetings for members of the board of directors, the right to bring a derivative suit and the right to receive certain dividends.

Shareholder's Agreement: Often done in small corporations, this is an agreement amongst shareholders that would allow one of the shareholders to take a management position within the corporation without claims of conflict of interest and/or self-dealing.

Shareholders' Derivative Suit: This is a lawsuit brought about by shareholders of a corporation, with the intent to protect the corporation against improper corporate management activity.

Shareholders' Meeting: Often held annually, this is a meeting of all shareholders to elect the board of directors of the corporation and to get reports on the company's current state of business.

Sharia: A series of principles and rules from Islamic law governing financial transactions, interest, speculation and unjust enrichment of one party over another.

Shell Company: A company that has no business or operations, but exists as a means to raise capital for future ventures or acquisitions.

Shirkah: In Islamic tradition, a partnership; a contract by parties to form a business, for example.

Single Joint Expert: While not allowed in some jurisdictions, one person is chosen or hired to present expert testimony instead of all parties to the action bringing in their own expert witnesses.

Single Member Company: In the United States, this may be a sole proprietor; a private company with limited shares and with only one principle.

Slip: A document used by an insurance broker to set out the details of the risk. If an underwriter agrees to accept the risk, the slip is signed and stamped and the risk is officially accepted.

Slip Rule: A court can correct clerical mistakes and accidental omissions in a judgment at any time if a party makes application for the changes.

Small Claims Court: see *below*

Small Claims Track: In the United Kingdom, for claims of 5,000 sterling or less, the rules and procedures are different and less formal. Recoverable costs are limited in small claims track. This is similar to the U.S. version of small claims court.

Smith, Adam: A Scottish thinker and author, he is considered the father of modern economics. His classic, *Wealth of Nations*, is a description of how economies operate in a free-market, without the intervention or interference of government. He lived from 1723 to 1790.

SMP: Acronym for Statutory Maternity Pay which requires an employer to pay maternity pay for all eligible workers.

Snagging List: In the United Kingdom, as a construction project nears completion, this is the list of items identified by the project manager or the architect which still need finishing. Final payment is typically withheld until this list is completed. In the United States, this list would be called a punch list or similar term.

Sole Proprietorship: A company that is owned by only one individual. Being one tax entity, the individual's and the business's profits and loses are taxed and reported on the individual's personal tax return.

Solvency: Where an individual or entity has enough funds to pay his/its debts (more assets than liabilities). Compare this with insolvency.

Some Other Substantial Reason (SOSR): In the United Kingdom, one of six fair reasons for dismissing an employee under the ERA 1996. In order for the dismissal to stand, the employer must prove that it acted reasonably and there was sufficient reason for dismissal.

Specific Performance: The right of a non-breaching party to a contract to demand that a breaching party perform the contract via an order by a judicial court. Although requiring the breaching party to pay money to the other party is an option, forcing performance will be done it the contract can still be performed and money would simply be insufficient.

Special Disclosure: In an attempt to resolve disputes, a court can order that a party go beyond an ordinary disclosure effort, looking for additional documents or something special or out of the ordinary.

Special Resolution: In the United Kingdom, 75 percent of shareholders need to vote in favor of a special resolution at the company's general meeting. This kind of resolution is required for such actions as changing the name of the company or altering the articles of the company.

Speculation: Risk taking out of proportion to realistic return.

SSP: Acronym for Statutory Sick Pay which requires an employer in the United Kingdom to pay any employee who is out of work because of illness after the first four days of absence up to 28 weeks.

Spring-loading: In the United Kingdom, an attempt by a company to advance executive options so that the holders can benefit from forthcoming or recent good news about the company. Under these circumstances, this action would be illegal and would be considered market abuse as the activity benefits only one class of investors. In the United States, this activity is similar to pre-dating options, which has been both controversial and illegal.

Springboard Injunction: A concept from the United Kingdom which concerns the use of confidential information by current or past employees. Basically, the injunction prevents an employee from using confidential information for his purposes and the courts provide relief to the company to prevent this abuse by an injunction.

Stamp Duty: In the United Kingdom it is a tax on financial instruments and certain written documents. As of 2003, stamp duty was applicable on shares, other marketable securities and some transactions involving partnerships.

Standard: A norm or level of excellent or performance. Standards in law, accounting, business operations, manufacturing and so forth.

Standard Basis: In the United Kingdom, courts will only allow costs which are proportionate to the matter at hand. This means that the part seeking to recover costs has to prove that the costs claimed are reasonable; this assumes that the party is not asking for costs on an indemnity basis.

Standard Dismissal and Disciplinary Procedure (Standard DDP): Under the Employment Act 2002 in the United Kingdom, a standard DDP involves the employer's written statement for grounds for dismissal; a meeting of both sides in which each can present it case; and an appeal meeting if requested by the employee.

Standing Interpretation Committee (SIC): This group is part of the International Accounting Standards Board (IASB) and its role is to rule on a timely basis about accounting issues that are likely to have different interpretations or treatment in the absence of some definitive statement.

Standstill Agreement: In the United Kingdom, this concept has a variety of meanings: It can restrict a shareholder from acquiring further stock during an attempted takeover; during a corporate restructuring, creditors give the company time to gather important information and research a survival strategy for the purpose of a formal restructuring.

State of Domicile: Often this refers to the state where a corporation is incorporated, and this usually is also where it is headquartered.

Statement of Case: In the United Kingdom these are the documents that a party uses to set out its case in a civil proceeding.

Statement of Truth: Generally language inserted into a formal document, such as an employment application, that confirms that the facts stated in the document are true. The document is then signed and witnessed.

Statements of Recommended Practice (SORPs): These statements supplement accounting standards and other legal and regulatory requirements; they tend to be applicable for specialized sectors, ones for which standard practices do not fit completely.

Statements of Standard Accounting Practice (SSAP): In the United Kingdom, the Accounting Standards Board (ASB) issues standards for accounting practice for public companies.

Statutory Demand: In the United Kingdom, this is a formal written demand for payment of a debt that is greater the 750 sterling. The payment must be received within 21 days. If the debt is not paid, the creditor can petition the court for relief.

Stay: This action puts a halt to any legal proceedings, apart from any steps allowed by the court during the term of the stay. The court activity will continue once the stay is lifted by the court.

Step-in Rights: If a developer in the United Kingdom becomes insolvent for whatever reason and is in breach of contract, another party may literally step in and complete the project, paying the first developer what is due, thus becoming the developer in his own right.

Sterling: Common term for British currency.

Stock Certificate: A written (printed) document stating ownership of shares in a corporation, while also listing the name of the corporation, the date and state of incorporation, the number of shares the certificate represents, the registered number of the certificate, names of shareholders, the issue date, and the total number of shares authorized in the particular issue of stock. Increasingly, stock certificates are no longer printed documents, but kept electronically, making it much easier to trade shares or transfer ownership.

Stock in Trade: A collection of goods/merchandise held for sale.

Straw Man: An individual who has been transferred a business interest with the sole purpose of concealing the true owner of the business. This individual has no part or participation within the business, but acts merely as a double for the real person that truly controls the business operations of a company. For example, a straw man may be put in place if the real owner is not permitted to act due to a criminal record.

Strike: Generally a work stoppage with the intention of disrupting normal business. Such activity is part of a labor/employer balancing act in an effort to get additional benefits, compensation or to preserve jobs. The threat of a work stoppage is usually enough for an employer to sit down with a union or workers' representatives to resolve any labor disputes.

Subcontractor: An individual or entity that contracts with a general contractor to perform some work that the general contractor has agreed to perform under a separate contract with another party. For example, in construction a drywall specialist may be a subcontractor on a job. A property owner, who had signed a contract with a general contractor, is responsible for making sure the general contractor pays all subcontractors and if payments are not made, the owner is still liable for what is due the subcontractors.

Subject Access Request: In the United Kingdom, under the Data Protection Act 1998 consumers have the right to access any of their personal data, such as credit history and financial information, help by third parties. Typically, there is a fee for services. In the United States, free access to credit histories is allowed once a year without charge.

Subordination: A series of loans are made to a corporation, and some are considered senior loans; they will be paid first before all other creditors. In addition, there may be other or junior loans; they will be paid last. These latter loans are subordinated to the first loan, thus the process of subordination. Variations on this theme exist in the U.S., the U.K. and in Europe.

Sub-prime Mortgage: This is a kind of real estate lending that does not conform to normal standards; often these mortgages are sold to individuals with a poor credit history or who have only a small down payment or may otherwise find it difficult to secure a conventional mortgage. The loans typically have a higher interest rate reflecting the higher risk of the lender.

Subrogate: In the insurance industry, for example, this is a remedy to prevent unjust enrichment. Assume that a company pays a claim to the insured; subrogation allows the insurer to recoup all or some of what was paid out from a third party who caused or contributed to the claim in the first place. In effect, the insurance company takes the place of the insured to reclaim losses caused by the third party in an effort to make itself whole.

Substantial Performance: In dealing with contracts, this is where almost all the obligations of a contract have been fulfilled, with a few minor variances or small defects that do not affect the outcome of the contract. For example, a clothing retailer ordered new packing boxes for its cloths and they were supposed to be delivered December 5, but did not arrive until December 26. This would constitute substantial performance, unless the boxes were to be used for a Christmas sale.

Subsidiary Company: A company that is controlled and/ or owned by another, parent company, either wholly or partly. The parent company holds the majority of the voting rights and can appoint or remove directors or managers as it sees fit.

Subsidy: Governmental or regional (as in the European Union) financial assistance for private companies. Subsidies can be direct (aid to farmers) or indirect (lower tax or incentives).

Sukuk: Similar to bonds, sukuks are financial instruments which do not violate Islamic laws and principles of sharia.

Sum Certain: A specific, set amount with a contract or negotiable instrument when the document is written that is not reliant on a future calculation or occurrence. A stated, set fee for doing work is an example of a sum certain, whereas, paying someone hourly is not.

Summary Dismissal: In the United Kingdom, this is an immediate firing of an employee without notice. This would normally be a breach of contract and not allowed except under unusual circumstances, such as gross misconduct.

Summary Judgment: A court can dismiss an action or find for a party to an action before an actual proceeding begins, based on the court's belief that there is no merit to the case and the claimant has no real prospects for success.

Surcharge: This is an additional charge applied to an original charge. It may result due to an omission from an original calculation, if terms have been changed due to some new circumstances, or because of some kind of penalty being applied. Airlines often add a fuel surcharge to the price of tickets when refined fuels prices increase dramatically.

Surrender: In the United Kingdom, this is a surrender of a lease by a tenant; typically it is a mutually agreed upon arrangement between the two parties to the lease.

Surety: Generally, a guarantor, whether a person or a company, that agrees to be responsible for the debts of others in the event of default.

SWIFT: Acronym for the Society of Worldwide Interbank Financial

Telecommunications. This is a secured computer system and software interface for financial institutions, banks and investment managers.

Swindle: Deliberate cheating or defrauding of another, with intent to gain an advantage which is not due.

Syndicate: A joint venture or an association of investors for some business purpose or project. All though it has a pejorative implication, it is a perfectly legitimate operation for the sake of business.

Syndicated Loan: One agreement is written by more than one bank to a credit line for a borrower or a group of borrowers. The process may be begun when one bank makes a loan and sells portions of the loan to other lenders, thus reducing its exposure (risk) of carring the full amount of the loan. One bank becomes the agent for all lenders to distribute payments of principal and interest.

T

Table A: In the United Kingdom, these are generic or model articles of association that automatically apply when a company is formed, assuming that the company does not adopt its own, specific articles of incorporation. Most private companies that are formed adapt the Table A articles as a means of saving money and for expediency.

Tag Along Rights: Protection for shareholders (usually minority owners) in a joint venture or private company whereby they can force the majority to seek offers for the shares of the company.

Take and Pay Contract: One party guarantees to purchase an agreed-upon amount of merchandise, as long as it is delivered. Alternatively, the purchaser agrees to pay the seller specific minimum payments even if delivery of the product is not taken.

Takeout Loans: Typically construction loans made by banks to finance commercial or industrial projects; the loan is written not to exceed 60 months in length. These loans are made with the knowledge that permanent or other long-term financing (bonds) are already in place.

Takeover: Acquisition of a business by another business or group of partners. This is accomplished by either buying the assets of the business or owning enough shares to control voting power and thus the board of directors. Takeovers can be hostile or friendly.

Talks Announcement: This is a possible offer announcement for the takeover of a company. The intent by the governing authorities on mergers and takeovers is to dampen speculation and thus prevent the price of shares from moving either higher or lower in extreme.

Tangible Property: Personal property that can be held and touched, as opposed to bank accounts and copyrights, which are examples of intangible property.

Take: Unproductive weight in shipping; for example, the weight of a barrel, crate or packaging in which the product is shipped. It is the difference between the gross weight and the net weight.

Taper Relief: In the United Kingdom, individuals, personal representatives and trustees can gain relief from capital gains tax; the relief is based on how long the asset sold has been held. There are different rates and different hold times for business assets as opposed to personal assets.

Tariff: A general term for a schedule of charges for services or merchandise. Can also mean the statutes under which duties on imports are imposed.

Tawarruq (Reverse Murabaha): Under Islamic law, this is a method whereby a financial institution buys an asset and immediately sells the asset to a customer on a deferral payment basis. The customer then sells the asset to a third party for cash while retaining the deferred payment basis with the bank.

Tax Avoidance: Legal efforts by corporations and individuals to reduce their respective tax liabilities; a tax shelter for example. Efforts make with the purpose of deception or by means disallowed by the courts or tax examiners are generally considered illegal. In recent years, taxing bodies have been increasingly aggressive with various tax avoidance schemes. If a plan is disallowed, the tax payer is responsible in most jurisdictions for not only the original tax due, but penalties and interest-both of which can be substantial.

Tax Credit: Any form of relief, for both businesses and individuals, which will directly or indirectly reduce the amount of tax owed. Depending up the individual country, tax credits can be applied for literally hundreds of items or events.

Taxflation: A term coined to reflect the increase in taxes because of inflation. The typical example is a tax on housing (some form of real estate tax) that is indexed to the value of the property. An owner may enjoy substantial appreciation on paper and thus a proportionately higher tax.

Tax Haven: Internationally recognized countries or municipalities that offer lower than average tax rates, thus encouraging investment. The end result is that companies and individuals pay less tax on their earnings than they would in their own country. Tax havens are notorious for their privacy laws and protection for investors. These secrecy laws can be broken, however, in the presence of illegal activities (money laundering) or crimes against humanity (stolen property during war time or money used for terrorism).

Tax Lien: The right to take, hold or otherwise dispose of property for the sake of satisfying a legitimate tax obligation. In most jurisdictions, filing for bankruptcy does not negate the tax lien.

Technical Provisions: Under the Pensions Act 2004 in the United Kingdom, the technical provisions of a salary-related pension scheme is the amount of reserves required to cover its liabilities.

Tenant: Any individual who is entitled for a period of time an interest in or possession of or occupation of an estate, usually in consideration of payment, such as rent. Under almost any jurisdiction, a tenant has a specific set of rights, even though he does not own or maintain title to the property. Conversely, the owner has expectations that the property will be maintained and returned in or a like condition when let to the tenant.

Tender: When dealing with contracts, this is to make an individual or entity an unconditional offer.

Tender Offer: This takes place when a company wishes to buy back its shares from shareholders; they are invited (offered) to tender their stock at a specific price or at the market price of the tender offer. In either case, the company will set a maximum as to the amount it is willing to pay for a tender offer.

Term: When dealing with contracts, this refers to both a period of time in which the contract is in force, as well as referring to a particular condition within the contract.

Term Loan: A borrower is allowed to draw down (borrow) a lump sum from the lender for a set period of time with an agreed repayment schedule. Once repaid, the amount cannot be re-borrowed.

Termination Agreement: In the case of employment, a signed document by the employee and the employer stating what benefits, pay and other forms of compensation will be paid to the employee and under what conditions their future relationship will be governed, e.g. a non-compete clause or a promise not to sue the employer. (These kinds of agreements will be governed by the labor laws of the country in which it is signed.) In contracts, this may be the terms and payments to be made by one party on termination of a contract.

Texas Shoot Out: This is a version of Russian roulette whereby either partners or shareholders in a business can serve notice on the other party to buy their shares or conversely sell its own shares to the other party at a specified price. The action, when taken, effectively ends the joint venture.

The Pensions Advisory Service (TPAS): A non-for-profit group in the United Kingdom whose sole role is to provide fee assistance to members of the public who have failed to resolve a pensions dispute with the trustees of a pension scheme.

Third Party: An individual that is not a named party to a contract, but who is involved in the contract dealings in some fashion (e.g., a witness to the contract signing). Often, these parties have no legal right to the contract dealings, unless the contract was entered into for his or her benefit.

Three Cs of Credit: Character, capacity and capital.

Thrift: A savings bank (formerly called savings and loan association) whose primary role is to collect deposits from savers and lend the money for residential mortgages and residential development. In the United Kingdom, this is similar to a building society.

Tier I Capital: Under the banking system in the United Kingdom, there are regulatory capital requirements to ensure that a bank maintains sufficient capital to absorb any losses it incurs as well as having sufficient funds to pay its liabilities and depositors on demand. Most countries with sophisticated banking laws have similar capital requirements; it is to the role of the bank examiners to ensure the financial stability of the institution.

Under the British system, there is also Tier 2 Capital and Tier3 Capital requirements, which included special reserves and a certain amount of subordinated debt to the capital structure of the bank.

Tight Money: Non-technical term for times of tight credit, sometimes even with quality collateral, borrowers end up being denied credit or offered credit with high interest rates.

Time Bill: A bill of exchange payable at some future date, say 90 days from the date of the bill.

Time Is of the Essence: A phrase often used in contracts to specify that a particular condition of the contract must be met as of a specified time and/or date. Being that the time and/or date becomes a vital component of the contract with this proviso; if it is not met it can be grounds for canceling the contract.

Time Value of Money: The notion that a future some of money will have less value than the same amount today because today's amount can be invested, and thus grow in value.

Tools of Trade: When dealing with bankruptcy, this refers to the tools or equipment an individual needs to work his or her occupation, and these tools are exempt from creditor claims.

Tombstone: A general announcement in the financial newspapers or professional publications whereby a company and its underwriter provides the basic details of a securities offerings and lists all the parties involved. It is not a solicitation for offers to buy.

Tort: A French phrase meaning wrong, this is the area of the law dealing with civil wrongs where injury occurs to another. This area of the law includes all intentional wrongs that result in harm, as well as negligence cases.

Tortious Measure of Damages: These are damages awarded as a result of a tort; the goal is to make the injured party whole, to put him back in the same position he was before the tort. Damages in tort are subject to the principles of remoteness, causation and mitigation.

Tracing: Any effort to find the real owner of personal or real property. Money can be traced nationally or internationally to determine the owner of money made or used for illegal purposes. Any traced money or assets have to be clearly disentangled from other money or assets. In the loan business, a variation (skip tracing) is an attempt to find debtors who have refused to pay their loans and seemingly are unable to be found in order to require or force payment.

Trade Dispute: In the United Kingdom particularly, any dispute between workers and their employers concerning terms or conditions of employment; suspension or termination of employment; work assignments; and/or membership or non-membership in a union.

Trade Name: This refers to the name of a business or a product that has a name and reputation so well known or used by the public that it is easily identifiable as that of a particular business. This is important, as use of a trade name for a similar or generic product made by another company can lead to an infringement action. Some names can loose their trade name status: cellophane, for example.

Trade Secret: A method, formula or other information distinctive and unique to a business that provides it with a competitive advantage, and as such, it has tremendous value to a business and can be protected by the court against employees, former employees or other individuals from divulging the trade secret. This is a business process and nor a patentable invention.

Trademark: A distinctive word, design, picture, phrase, logo, or other type of symbol or wording used by businesses to differentiate and set apart its product(s) from its competitors. Trademarks may be registered with the U.S. Patent Office and use of another's trademark can be the basis for an infringement lawsuit.

Transfer Agent: A company or individual hired by a corporation to process the transfer and registration of stock.

Transfer Pricing: Within companies with multiple divisions, the prices at which goods, services and other assets are transferred/sold to other business entities within the corporation. While transfer prices are typically lower than what would be offered to a company's best customer, they must follow some reasonable standard and be recorded as real transactions.

Transactions at an Undervalue: In the course of a company liquidation or bankruptcy, the administrator may petition the court for an order voiding any transaction that was substantially undervalued in the previous two years.

Transferable Security: In the United Kingdom under the Financial Services and Markets Act 2000, any instruments other than money market instruments, which can be sold on a public market, can be transferable: shares, partnerships, depository receipts, bonds, securitized debt or any other instrument which can be settled for cash.

Transparency International: A non-governmental agency active in 70 countries and based in Berlin, Germany whose goal is to reduce international bribery and corruption in business and financial dealings.

TRAX: Acronym for The International Securities Market Association (ISMA) in 1989 created TRAX as a risk management, trade matching and regulatory reporting system for facilitating trading in the financial markets.

Treasurer: The corporate officer who is responsible for granting and obtaining credit, collecting and depositing money and general cash disbursements.

Treasury Bill: Issued in multiples of $10,000 by the United Stated Treasury, this is a promissory note that has a maturity date of not more than a year.

Treasury Consent: In the United Kingdom, before a company can carry out certain transactions involving their overseas subsidiaries, the companies are required to seek permission from Treasury before taking the intended actions. The overall goal is to ensure that there is not a loss of tax to the British government as a result of these transactions.

Treasury Stock: These are stocks that were originally issued, but have now been reacquired by the corporation. While these stocks do earn the corporation dividends, they do not grant voting rights.

Trehandanstalt: Germany's 1990s policies for privatizing companies and assets in the former East Germany.

Trust: A business combination which controls a large number of assets, often with the idea of eliminating competition. Also, a fiduciary responsibility to hold or manage property or an estate on behalf of another.

Trustee in Bankruptcy: The individual or group that takes charge of personal or business assets of the bankrupt, whose primary duty is arrange for the sale of all assets at the best price and to distribute those assets to the creditors according to an agreed upon schedule of disbursement.

Truth in Lending Act: A requirement that commercial lenders (e.g. bank, mortgage brokers) provide a potential borrower with accurate information regarding interest rates, due dates and a three-day period so he or she can look at competitive rates or to cancel the loan all together.

TUPE: Acronym for Transfer of Undertakings Protection of Employment Regulations 2006. In the United Kingdom this legislation regulates the transfer of employees from one entity to another when a company is sold.

Turnover: Sales turnover of merchandise.

Turnbull Report: Published by the Institute of Chartered Accountants of England and Wales, it provides assistance and direction to officers and directors of listed companies in the United Kingdom with respect to ensuring that companies have proper internal controls on significant matters of risk management for their respective companies.

Turnkey Contract: A full-service agreement between two parties whereby the vendor will take full responsibility for the set-up and management of an operation for the customer. Classic examples are computer systems and communications (phone) systems; the notion is that the customer has to merely turn the key and everything operates as expected. Such contracts are used when a company does not have the internal ability to build a customized system.

Tying or Tie-in: An agreement or arrangement where one item is tied to another; making the purchase of one product conditional on the purchase of another product. A store wants to sell one line of products, but must take the entire line to get the one it wants.

U

***Uberrimae Fidei*:** Literally from the Latin for utmost good faith. Insurance contracts, for example, are governed under this principle.

UCC-1: A financing agreement form that-under the provisions of the Uniform Commercial Code (UCC)-allows a borrower to secure a loan by using personal property as loan security.

U.K. GAAP: Acronym for Generally Accepted Accounting Principles in the United Kingdom; there is no formal definition as to what this is as the rules have been changed. Generally it is understood to mean that a public company is complying with U.K. law, accounting standards and generally best practices.

Ultra Vires: Latin phrase meaning beyond powers, this term is used to denote when a corporation's or its officers' conduct goes well beyond those powers granted by the law, as well as against its company's objectives.

Unassented Securities: Stocks or bonds which a corporation attempts to change their status, but the owners have not or will not agree to the change.

Unauthorized Payment: In the United Kingdom, a payment not permitted by the Finance Act 2004 made by a registered pension scheme.

Unconscionable: When dealing with contract law, this refers to a situation where an agreement is so unfair and/or so weighted against one party that no reasonable individual would agree to its terms. A court will not enforce, and subsequently will terminate, a contract where unconsionability can be shown.

Undercapitalization: Where a company lacks sufficient funds/cash to continue operating its business. This is a common problem with new ventures or companies which are growing rapidly-they literally can grow themselves into bankruptcy because the capital structure underlying the business is not sufficient for its growth rate.

Underground Economy: A shadow or hidden economy, whether legal or not, in which goods and services are produced but never reported, for tax or other purposes. Part-time work for which no taxes are deducted; sales of illegal drugs.

Underwater Option: An employee's option to shares that is out of the money, meaning that the price the employee has to pay for the shares of stock under the option is greater than the current market value of the shares. If he exercises the option, he bought shares at a greater price that he could have by not exercising his option. In the 1990s, options in high-technology companies were granted in huge numbers to recruit and maintain important employees. Often by the time the options could be exercised, they were worthless because the value of the stock had decreased to a price less than the option price.

Underwriter: A person or enterprise which offers any kind of insurance contracts for payment. Alternatively, this is a financial institution which helps companies with the sale of stocks or other securities.

Uniform Customs and Practice for Documentary Credits (UCP): The International Chamber of Commerce (ICC) issues an international set of rules concerning the rights and obligations of traders and bankers concerning letters of credit.

Undisclosed Principal: An individual that utilizes the services of an agent for his or her negotiations with a third party. This often makes it appear the agent is acting for himself or herself, and so the third party may not know who the real principal is if a dispute arises.

Unfair Competition: Utilizing fraudulent business practices to gain an unfair business advantage over competitors. Examples of this include using deceptive advertisements, confusing the public by utilizing imitative trademarks or packaging and/or maliciously disparaging another company's product through falsity.

Uniform Commercial Code (UCC): A set of laws in the United States covering commercial business transactions, the conduct of businesses, as well as other commercial matters. The UCC has been adopted by most states.

Unilateral Contract: A different type of contract in that it does not require a promise in exchange for a promise, but rather, this type of agreement requires payment in exchange for performance, if, and only if, the individual contracted to perform chooses to perform. For example, I will pay you $500.00 if pick up my mother from St. Louis and drive her to Chicago. The act of transporting the mother is acceptance.

Union Shop: Where a majority of workers vote to have a union represent them as their certified bargaining agent.

Unissued Stock: Shares of a corporation that have never been sold (issued) to anyone, in spite of the fact that they have been authorized by the corporation's articles of incorporation.

Unit Trust: An open-ended fund whose goal is to allow investors to acquire a small stake in a large number of publicly traded companies; the assumption is that the market risk will be spread over a large number of companies or sectors, so if one company or group of stocks goes down in value, it does not affect adversely the overall performance of the unit trust.

Unjust Enrichment: An improper gain or benefit of another's property or money by one that has not worked or paid for it, and who should not keep it. Often the recipient is required to return the property to its owner, even if not obtained in an illegal manner.

Unsecured Debt: This is when money is borrowed based solely on the general credit of a borrower, without the aid and security of said borrower pledging specific assets to be forfeited if repayment is not made. The creditor must sue and get a judgment to collect unpaid loans.

Urgent Issues Task Force (UITF): In the United States, the Accounting Standards Board (ASB) has formed a committee to deal with urgent accounting issues on an ad hoc basis. The committee's published abstracts must be followed by corporations and are part of the ASB's rules and regulations.

U.S. Person: Under Regulation S, Securities and Exchange Commission (SEC), any natural person resident in the United States. The definition expands to include any partnership or corporation organized under U.S. laws. It can also be defined as any estate, trust or fiduciary.

U.S. Reporting Issuer: A company that is registered under the Securities Exchange Act of 1934 and is required under the act to file periodic reports with the SEC.

Usury: When dealing with debts, this is an interest rate that is excessive and well above the percentage allowed by law. If a court finds an interest rate is usurious it will not enforce payment of the interest on the debt.

Utility Patent: A type of patent that lasts for 20 years (from the patent application filing date) and is issued for an invention that carries out a useful function.

V

Valuable Consideration: An essential part of contract formation that allows a benefit to be conferred upon the other party. Examples of valuable consideration include: money, a promise, performance, etc.

Valeurs: French equivalent to the word securities; stock are called actions and bonds are obligations

Valorization: An arbitrary market value for a commodity in part established by government interference in the free market. In the past, Brazil has attempted to keep the price of coffee high through various schemes.

Value: The monetary worth of something, its marketable price or what it has been estimated to be worth; a fair price.

Value Added Tax: A system used in most European countries, it is a tax on almost every good or service produced and is used as a general revenue fund.

***Verba Fortius Accipiuntur Contra Proferentem*:** A Latin phrase/expression that is a principal of contract construction, and indicates that if the words in a contract seem to be ambiguous, of two equally possible meanings, the meaning of the word(s) should be interpreted against the author of the word(s), and not against the other party to the contract.

Venture Capital: Seed money or funds provided for start-up businesses, often small and high-risk ventures, which are perceived to have high profit potential at some future time. Venture capital is most commonly associated with high technology industries.

Verification: In the context of issuing stock or shares in a company, it is the process of ensuring that the documents produced as part of the stock issuance are accurate, true and not misleading. It is the responsibility of the directors (with the help of their advisors) to ensure that the documents are free from flaws.

Vertical Integration: A business arrangement seen less and less, but essentially a single business entity that supplies (manufacturers) also does the distribution and sells directly to the consumer. The oil and gas industry is an example, whereby the crude is pumped, refined, distributed and sold by the same company.

Vicarious Liability: Often referred to as imputed liability, in business this is where an employee, who has negligently caused injury to another while working within the scope of employment, can impute liability to his or her employer and cause the employer to be liable for damages.

Victimization: Generally any type of discrimination against an individual, treating that individual less favorably than others, because the individual has made a discrimination claim or given evidence in connection to a discrimination claim.

Vise: An official endorsement on a document such as a passport attesting to its validity. The term visa is used in the United States.

Void: When dealing with contracts, this is when an agreement becomes null and has no effect. For example, a mutually rescinded contract is void and cancelled.

Voidable: Different from void, (which means never existed), this refers to a situation where a contract is capable of being made void. For example, a contract entered into by a minor is voidable when he or she reaches the age of majority, but it can also be affirmed when he or she reaches the age of majority.

***Volenti Non Fit Injuria*:** A Latin phrase meaning, the volunteer suffers no wrong. This is often used within a tort/civil lawsuit and means that one who consents to an activity which caused him or her damages, cannot then turn around and make a claim against another for those damages.

Voting Trust: A trust that seeks the vote proxies of shareholders of a corporation in order to elect a board of directors, as well as to vote on other matters at a shareholder's meeting.

Voucher: A receipt or a written evidence of an expenditure or payment of a debt. A cancelled check is often considered a voucher because it is Used for proof of payment.

W

Wages: Any sum of money paid or payable to a worker in regards to employment. Typically, holiday pay, salary, bonuses, commissions, sick pay and other related payments are lumped under the term wages.

Warehouse Receipt: When an individual that stores goods for hire issues a receipt to the person or entity storing those goods. This document constitutes a document of title under the UCC, so the person holding the document has clear tile to receive the goods.

Warranty: A written statement that signals the good quality of a product or merchandise, as well as to signal that a fact stated within a contract is true.

Wasting Assets: Minerals, coal, oil or timber or other natural resources which are depleted as the source is mined or worked.

Watered Stock: Shares of a corporation that have been issued at a price that is greater than the actual current value of the shares. This is often indicated within a corporations accounts.

Whistleblowing: Generally reporting that a manager or an employer is engaged in illegal, dangerous or questionable behavior; typically, the report can be made within the company, to outside legal advisors, to regulators or even to a spiritual advisor. There are legal protections on the books to protect whistleblowers.

White Elephant: Quaint term for any property or business which is either obsolete or cannot be operated for a profit and can only be sold at a huge loss. An aging warehouse needing a great deal of repair in an economically depressed area is a white elephant.

White Collar Crime: A term often referring to crimes done by business executives rather than blue collar workers, these crimes include: commercial fraud, swindles, insider trading, embezzlement and other dishonest business plots. These crimes, however, can be committed by anyone, at any level of a business.

White Knight: In takeover situations, in order to prevent being bought out, a company may bring in another bidder as an alternative to the current buyer as a means of voiding the takeover by the current bidder.

White Squire: Any individual who has taken (purchased) a large stake in a company by buying existing shares or new shares in an offering; the acquired stake is large enough to block any hostile takeover bid.

Winding up: This refers to a process that occurs before a corporation or partnership comes to an end, and involves liquidating assets, paying outstanding bills, settling accounts and distributing the remaining assets to shareholders or partners and then dissolving the business.

Window Dressing: Corporate practice of temporarily making the business look better than it actually is. If the intent is to defraud (realize a higher price) then the practice is illegal.

Without Prejudice: A settlement is reached and is written down for all parties. The documents would be marked without prejudice-the purpose is to protect one or both parties from embarrassing statements in the documents made purely in an attempt to settle a matter.

Witness Order: In the United Kingdom labor environment, an employment tribunal may issue an order that a person is required to attend a meeting; failure to attend is a criminal offense

Wolfsberg Group: A group of international, money center banks that has banned together to promote the international fight against the financing of terrorism.

Work Made for Hire: This is work that an employee completes while working within the scope of employment, and for copyright purposes, if the company employing the employee commissions the work, then the company is the owner and author of the material, as well as the copyright, not the individual that actually created the work.

Workers' Compensation Acts: These are statutes established by states which set up certain levels of liability of employers for injuries or illnesses sustained by workers while on the job. Employers in states with workers' compensation statutes must provide insurance to protect workers, and if granted to an employee it becomes the only remedy against an employer, and restricts the worker or his or her family from bringing lawsuits against the employer from the injury or death of the worker. Some employees may waive workers' compensation, and he or she can then sue his or her employer for damages.

Work in Process: Inventory which is partially assembled, but not finished by the end of the reporting period. The materials are the least liquid because they are neither parts nor fully-assembled inventory.

Workout Loans: Problem loans placed on a work-out basis, e.g. borrowers are given additional time to work out of their financial difficulties and work towards full repayment of the outstanding loan sometime in the future.

Write Off: Reducing the value of an asset, loan or inventory, for example, to reflect the real economic value if the item were to be sold. Banks write off loans when it appears that they will never be paid. Obsolete inventory (or inventory parts) is written off because they no longer have the stated book value.

Write Up: The opposite of write off or write down, meaning a new value is assigned to assets or inventory which have increased in value. Generally not encouraged as good business practice, it may be a means of window dressing. Accounting and business standards always encourage the most conservative valuation of assets on the books.

Wrongful Termination: If a court rules that termination from a job was illegal, then the employee has the right to sue the employer from this wrongful discharge, and he or she can seek lost wages and benefits damages, and possibly punitive damages as well. In order for the terminated employee to be successful, the discharge must have not been for "cause," and the employee must have had either: a written or implied contract which provided reasons to believe the employment would be permanent; there must have discriminatory reasons for the discharge; or the discharge must have been contrary to "public policy."

Y-Z

Yellow-Dog Contracts: These are unenforceable contracts in which an employer prohibits an employee from joining a labor union.

Yield: This refers to the current return rate (as a percentage) of the price of a stock or bond. For example, if a stock sells for $35.00 and pays a dividend of $1.75, then the yield is five percent (5%).

Zombie Thrifts: Insolvent savings banks (or savings and loan associations) which have been placed with the Federal Deposit Insurance Corporation (FDIC) for management.

Zone of Employment: This refers to the physical area in which if an employee gets injured those injuries are compensable under worker' compensation laws.

Zoning: A restriction on certain lands (often by local governments) for particular uses, such as for: commercial use, agricultural use, single-family residential use, schools and other purposes.